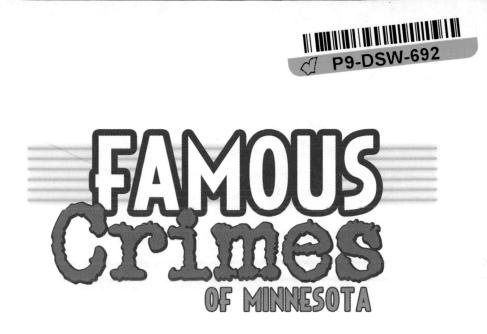

FAMOUS Crimes OF MINNESOTA

by Michael Burgan

Adventure Publications
Cambridge, Minnesota

Dedication

In loving memory of my father, Bernard Burgan, a one-time small town cop who taught me that crime does not pay.

Acknowledgments

Writing a book like this means standing on the shoulders of giants—the crime reporters who gave readers the facts as the stories unfolded, and the writers who explored the stories in greater depth for later books. While the bibliography notes my key sources, I want to single out several authors and their works: Walter Trenerry, for his *Murder in Minnesota*; Paul Maccabee for his seminal *Dillinger Slept Here*; and Larry Millett, for *Murder Has a Face*. I'd also like to thank the staff at the Minnesota Historical Society, where I had the chance to go over some of Maccabee's research materials, which now form the society's St. Paul Gangster History Research Collection. I also received useful assistance from the staff at the University of Minnesota's Wilson Library. Finally, I'd like to thank a few people by name: Blake Hoena, who first proposed this project; Russell Primm, who encouraged me to take it on; Hampton Smith at the MHS, who recommended some key resources; Jack El-Hai, who suggested some contemporary crimes to include; Brett Ortler, my editor at Adventure Publications; and Sharon Jennings, who took care of my cat while I traveled to Minnesota.

Photo credits: Minnesota House of Representatives: 7 Library of Congress: 12, 13, 14 National Archives: 28 Courtesy of The Minnesota Historical Society: 38, 41, 45, 53, 55, 81, 91, 125 Flickr User Shannon Mollerus: 44 Star Tribune: 46, 87, 89, 92, 95, 99, 104, 106, 109, 112, 117, 154, 157 Courtesy of the FBI: 52, 56, 57, 59, 60 (both), 63 (both), 64, 66 (all), 71, 72, 75, 78 (both), 80 (both), 137, 138, 150, 165 Courtesy of Wofford College, Littlejohn Collection: 76 Flickr User Hollyberrie05: 97 Courtesy of *Killed in the Line of Duty*: 100 Courtesy of Wikipedia user Bobak Ha'Eri: 102 Minnesota Department of Corrections: 119, 121, 135, 142, 149 Courtesy of Flickr User Lomiere: 131 Courtesy of Flickr User Drumminghands: 166 All other photos are public domain.

Front cover photos: Left: Public domain. Middle: Courtesy of Wofford College, Littlejohn Collection. Right: Flickr User Lomiere.

Back cover photos: Left: Library of Congress. Right: Courtesy of the FBI. Bottom: Courtesy of the FBI.

The photos on pages 44, 97, 102, 123, 166 and the front cover photo on the right-hand side are licensed under the Creative Commons Attribution License, which is available here: http://creativecommons.org/licenses/by/3.0/us/

Cover and book design by Jonathan Norberg

Table of Contents

FROM STATEHOOD TO THE GANGSTER ERA

A Husband's Slow Death 5
A Robbery Gone Wrong. 13
The Murder of Kitty Ging 21
Family Matters 29
The Wife Gets It 33
The Circus Lynchings 38
When the Criminal Becomes the Victim 46
A Favorite Madam 50
Willmar Bank Robbery 57
Snatching Millionaires 64
One Who Got Away. 72
Beating the Rap–As Usual 81

THE POST-WAR ERA TO THE DAWN OF THE NEW MILLENNIUM

Robbery Leads to Murder 87
The Dentist Did It 92
The Family That Slays Together 99
This Gun For Hire 104
One Mother's Cruelty, Another's Love 112
Racial Tensions of the Times 119
Paying a High Price. 123
A Murder in the Family 128
Obsession Turns Violent. 135
Murder on the Farm. 142
A Mystery Resolved 150
The Angry Heir 154
A Cold Case of Murder 161

OTHER NOTABLE MINNESOTA CRIMES 165

CHAPTER NOTES 168

INDEX 179

ABOUT THE AUTHOR 184

From Statehood to the Gangster Era

A Husband's Slow Death. 5

A Robbery Gone Wrong 13

The Murder of Kitty Ging. 21

Family Matters. 29

The Wife Gets It 33

The Circus Lynchings 38

When the Criminal Becomes the Victim 46

A Favorite Madam 53

Willmar Bank Robbery 57

Snatching Millionaires 64

One Who Got Away 72

Beating the Rap—As Usual 81

A Husband's Slow Death

THE CRIME: A shopkeeper dies after a long illness, with poison later determined to be the cause of death

VICTIM: Stanislaus Bilansky

PERPETRATOR: Bilanksy's wife, Ann, is convicted and executed for the crime

SCENE OF THE CRIME: St. Paul

WHEN: Death occurred March 11, 1859; Mrs. Bilansky is hung on March 23, 1860

Minnesotans had just celebrated achieving statehood a few months before Stanislaus Bilansky tied the knot for the third time, in September 1858. In his early 50s, he might not have seemed like much of a catch: Short and squat, he tended toward hypochondria, and friends attested that he could be a nasty drunk. But something attracted Mary Ann Evards Wright to the former tailor-turned-shopkeeper, who had first settled in St. Paul in 1842.

Unlike her husband, Wright was a recent arrival, a widow who had come to town at the invitation of her nephew, John Walker. Ann was known for her prominent front teeth, gray eyes, intelligence and high energy. Moving in with her new husband on Stillwater Street, she seemed a good stepmother to his three children. The family was completed when Walker moved into a spare cabin behind the Bilansky house shortly after the couple were married.

Stanislaus, though, did not have much time to enjoy his new marital bliss—if it was blissful at all. He fell ill in December 1858, recovered, then suffered a new ailment toward the end of February. He was soon bedridden, complaining of stomach pains and a fever. A neighbor, Lucinda Kilpatrick, later recalled his frequent, severe vomiting spells: "I have known him to vomit three times in half an hour."[1] Bilansky was not under a doctor's care until March 5, after he seemed to take a turn for the worse. But the doctor wasn't too concerned. His prescription—some absinthe mixed with water at mealtime. Bilansky also self-medicated with Graffenburg pills, which one advocate of the patent medicine claimed could cure everything from cholera to a hangnail.

Despite the doctor's prescription and the Graffenburgs, Bilansky died several days later. With assistance from her nephew, Ann Bilansky arranged for her husband's burial on March 12. Before the coffin could be placed in the ground, however, the Ramsey County coroner's office held an inquest. After searching the house and questioning a few people, the inquest ended and the funeral went on as planned. But by Sunday night, Ann Bilansky and John Walker were in jail, under suspicion for the murder of Stanislaus Bilansky. As the *Pioneer & Democrat* reported on March 15, what had first been considered a natural death, "caused by the ordinary habit of the man, and his own obstinacy, and carelessness," had become a case of suspected murder. The paper reported that "*. . . He had been poisoned, and that . . . poison had been administered by his wife.*"[2]

A NEIGHBOR'S SUSPICIONS

Mrs. Kilpatrick had been one of the people questioned the day of Bilansky's funeral. After first saying she hadn't noticed anything odd in her neighbors' home, she went back to officials with another story. She had gone shopping with Ann Bilansky several weeks before, and the woman had bought arsenic, ostensibly to kill rats that had been plaguing the root cellar ever since the departure of the family cat. Based on that testimony, Bilansky's body was exhumed, the arrests were made, and a second coroner's inquest was scheduled.

At that time, Kilpatrick added more details about her shopping expedition with the widow and murder suspect. Kilpatrick said that Mrs. Bilansky had asked her to buy the arsenic, but Kilpatrick had refused. After Bilansky's death, Ann also supposedly asked Kilpatrick to say she had bought the arsenic. The neighbor replied that Ann had nothing to worry about, if she hadn't poisoned her husband. But Ann thought that Stanislaus might have taken it himself, and she would be blamed. (As it later turned out, Stanislaus had something of an obsession about death, telling his second wife that he was sure he would die in March. And some claims surfaced that Bilansky had contemplated—or even attempted—suicide after his divorce from that wife.)

Kilpatrick said she didn't know much about family life in the Bilansky household, except what Ann had told her: "She said they lived unhappily; she hated him, and could not treat him well."[3] The family doctor, Alfred Berthier, offered his views on the marital relationship of the Bilanskys. Stanislaus told the doctor he was upset about Walker, the nephew, living so close by. "He thought there was an improper intimacy between his wife and Walker."[4] The press had already reported a similar story about the close relationship between the putative nephew and aunt.

MN House of Representatives

Gallows scene in Minnesota's early days

Rosa Scharf also offered key testimony that painted Ann Bilansky into a dark corner. Scharf had been hired on March 2 to help look after Stanislaus. She said she had never seen any arsenic in the house—but she hadn't noticed any rats either. She first said relations between the spouses were good, but then the next minute Scharf stated that Ann treated her husband "in a rough manner" during his illness.[5] And on the day of the funeral, Scharf testified, Mrs. Bilansky told her that "if Mr. B was poisoned, he had poisoned himself."[6] With the testimony from witnesses and a preliminary medical report that suggested the presence of arsenic, Ann Bilansky was formally charged with murder. John Walker, meanwhile, was released.

A Concealed "Weapon"

For people, often women, seeking revenge or hoping to eliminate an unwanted human obstacle to love or riches, poisoning—in cumulative doses or one mammoth shot—has a long history. Whatever their motive, women throughout history have often had plenty of opportunities, in their roles as cooks and dispensers of medicine. Poison was used in ancient Rome to remove rivals or advance the political career of loved ones. In France, arsenic was often the chemical of choice for wives hoping to get rich quick, and the poison earned the nickname "inheritance powder." In more recent days, a group of Ukrainian Jews who survived the Nazi Holocaust spiked bread with arsenic. The bread was meant for SS guards awaiting trial for their atrocities. Ann Bilansky's case seems to join the long list of murders-by-poison—if she were truly guilty.

THE TRIAL BEGINS

On May 23, 1859, Ann Bilansky entered the small, brick building that served as St. Paul's first courthouse. Defending her against the murder charge was John Brisbin, a Yale graduate who had become active in local politics since settling in St. Paul. Opposing him was district attorney Isaac V. D. Heard, another recent transplant from the east. The twelve men chosen as the jury included Justus C. Ramsey, brother of Minnesota's first territorial governor, Alexander Ramsey. The former governor would return to head the state's executive branch the next year—in time to immerse him in the Bilansky case.

WOMAN HANGED IN EARLY DAYS

MRS. BILANSKY FIRST WHITE PERSON EXECUTED IN STATE.

No Other Case Known in Minnesota History—The Law Permits a Reprieve for Special Reason Existing in Brennan Case, but Doesn't Remit the Penalty.

Some familiar faces from the coroner's inquest appeared during the trial as key witnesses for the prosecution. Lucinda Kilpatrick repeated her claim that Ann Bilansky had bought arsenic and made comments that hinted at murder. But what emerged for the first time was the possibility that Kilpatrick had her own intimate interest in John Walker, whom the prosecution claimed had no family ties to Mrs. Bilansky. Kilpatrick refused to answer many of the defense's questions about her various relations, but she did allow that the "friendly terms" between her and Walker "were broken up over a month ago."[7] Brisbin also presented physical evidence that linked her and Walker; once again she refused to comment on it, and the judge sustained most of the prosecution's objections.

Rosa Scharf also testified again, and this time spoke about the improper way—to her mind—that Mrs. Bilansky treated her husband. She also tried to suggest sexual impropriety between Bilansky and Walker, though cross-examination dampened that claim. The evidence also included more scientific assertions from several doctors that they found signs of arsenic in Stanislaus Bilansky's body. Under Brisbin's dogged questioning, they had to admit they had no particular expertise that could buttress their observations. And Dr. William Morton, who led the medical team, allowed that the seemingly miraculous Graffenburg pills could be fatal if someone took a large quantity at once.

THE DEFENSE MOVES IN

When the time came for the defense to present its case, Attorney Brisbin was sick, so another lawyer on the team, a Mr. Williams, stepped in. Defense witnesses included Stanislaus Bilansky's second wife, Ellen Truett, who portrayed her former husband as a man prone to violence when drunk—and he was often drunk. Truett also said that the third Mrs. Bilansky had bawled after the funeral, a contrast to the more heartless view of the defendant presented by others. One of Bilansky's sons, Benjamin, also took the stand. He confirmed the invasion of rats in the house that began after the departure of the family cat, which Stanislaus had given away. The ten-year-old also said he never saw any improper interaction between his stepmother and John Walker.

Walker also testified, affirming his family relationship with Ann Bilansky. He said their conduct together had always been proper, and that she had treated her late husband well.

By the time final arguments came, Brisbin was back in court, and he focused on the circumstantial nature of the state's evidence. There was no solid medical proof that Mr. Bilansky had died of poisoning, or if he had, that Ann had dosed him. His arguments, however, didn't sway the jury, which needed just five hours to find Ann Bilansky guilty of murder in the first degree. Brisbin appealed, seeking a new trial, but lost in the state Supreme Court. Among other arguments, the Court rejected Brisbin's theory that Lucinda Kilpatrick was out to frame Ann Bilansky, because of the former's relationship with John Walker.

THE ROAD TO THE GALLOWS

On July 25, 1859, the news came down that sentencing for Ann Bilansky would go forward. That night, Ann was momentarily out of her cell and away from her jailer's watchful eye. She bolted downstairs, found a way through an open window, and sped out into the night. Now a fugitive, she headed for Lake Como and hid in the area for several days, then contacted the one person she felt she could trust: John Walker. He brought her men's clothes to wear as a disguise, but the ruse was soon over, as county deputies spotted them and brought them back to St. Paul.

At the sentencing trial on December 2, Bilansky continued to assert her innocence, and she questioned if justice had been served during the first trial. The judge ordered her held in solitary confinement for one month, and then had her wait for incoming governor Alexander Ramsey to set the date for her execution. When the judge finished speaking, the convicted murderer cried hysterically.

Governor Ramsey had stepped into a judicial cause célèbre that sparked hundreds of letters and a bill from the state legislature that would commute Bilansky's sentence. Some people were appalled that the state would execute a woman, while others accepted the argument that she did not receive a fair trial. Historian Matthew Cecil has suggested that the governor might have had personal and political reasons for resisting the commutation of the capital sentence. He might upset voters, and the Republican might bring a positive glow to the defense attorneys, who were Democrats. Also, his brother, Justus

Ramsey, had played a part in finding Bilansky guilty, and he might have tried to influence his governor brother. As the execution date of March 23, 1860, drew closer, Ramsey wrote in his journal about the "annoyance" he felt because of the letters he received on Bilansky's behalf.[8]

The concerns over the lawfulness of the execution even touched the man who had prosecuted Bilansky. District Attorney Heard wrote the governor on March 22 that he had "grave and serious doubts as to whether the defendant has had a fair trial."[9] Still, the execution went on as planned.

On March 23, Ann Bilansky walked out of her cell, dressed in black. A reporter noted that she "walked through the hall with a firm step."[10] A day earlier, she had said that Lucinda Kilpatrick and Rosa Scharf had lied, often, on the stand. Scharf was not around to challenge that claim; she had killed herself several months before. Today some speculate that the suicide resulted from the guilt Scharf felt for her role in Bilansky's conviction.

On the gallows, Bilansky prayed for a few minutes. Then, rising from her knees, she gave her last statement. She said, in part, "I die without having any mercy shown me, or justice . . . I die a sacrifice to the law. I hope you all may be judged better than I have been, and by a more righteous judge." As the hangman stepped forward with the rope, she asked him, "How can you stain your hands by putting that rope around my neck—the instrument of my death?"[11] He replied he was just doing his job.

A contemporary account of Bilansky's hanging

With the hanging, Ann Bilansky became the first person executed in the state of Minnesota—and the only woman to meet that fate. Today, the Bilansky case has the sensational appeal of poisoning, adultery and betrayal. It also raises questions over whether justice was truly served—a particular concern in a trial featuring a capital offense. Minnesota allowed executions until 1911.

ANOTHER NOTABLE MINNESOTA CRIME

1862 DAKOTA UPRISING

In the early 1860s, relations between American Indians and settlers were tense. An all-out war was triggered after an incident when some young Indian hunters argued with a settler and then killed him and some of his neighbors. Tribal war leaders saw the incident as a way to take a stand against white encroachment, rather than wait for the U.S. government to exact some form of retribution. They convinced Little Crow, a Sioux chief, to sanction the war, which he reluctantly did. In August 1862, fighting took place around Fort Ridgley and in late September, the U.S. military had established control and began conducting military tribunals. The Indians were not formally charged with crimes but were asked to explain their role in the war. Simply firing a gun during a battle, whether the shot killed anyone or not, led to a warrior's guilt and a death sentence. President Lincoln commuted many of those sentences to prison terms, but in the largest mass execution in U.S. history, 38 Indians were hanged in Mankato for their role in the uprising.

Library of Congress

A lithograph of the hanging scene

A Robbery Gone Wrong

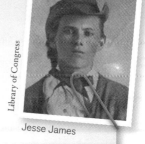

THE CRIME: A botched robbery leads to the death of several people and the capture of three members of the James-Younger Gang

PERPETRATORS: Jesse and Frank James; Cole, Jim and Bob Younger; Bill Chadwell; Charlie Pitts; Clell Miller

VICTIMS: Joseph Heywood; Nicholas Gustafson

SCENE OF THE CRIME: Robbery in Northfield; capture near Madelia

WHEN: Robbery on September 7, 1876; capture on September 21, 1876

Library of Congress

Jesse James

In the years after the Civil War, the legend of Jesse James and his outlaw gang filled newspapers and served as the inspiration for poems and songs. James helped create the legend himself, writing letters to newspapers in between his crimes, sometimes denying them, other times painting himself as a Robin Hood who gave his ill-gotten gains to the poor. (Of course, he and those who made him into some sort of folk hero ignored the fact that the stolen money often belonged to hard-working common people, and not the "one percent" of the day.)

In 1876, James, his brother Frank, and the rest of their gang ventured out of their usual area of criminal activity. They targeted the First National Bank in Northfield, Minnesota, with politics as well as money in mind. The gang heard that Adelbert Ames, former governor of Mississippi, and his father-in-law General Benjamin Butler had just deposited $75,000 in the bank. Ames had recently moved to Northfield to take over his aging father's flour mill. The deposit, though, may have just have been a rumor, as some say it never occurred.

To the James gang, the two Northerners were justifiable targets for robbery, given their treatment of Southerners during and after the Civil War. Most of the gang had fought under William Quantrill, leader of Quantrill's Raiders, an infamous Confederate group that carried out guerrilla warfare in Kansas and nearby states. To James and the others, Ames was a carpetbagger who represented the Radical Reconstruction carried out by vengeful Republicans. Butler, in the mind of Cole Younger, was especially deserving of being robbed, after his harsh treatment of the citizens of New Orleans during the war. Younger later wrote, "We felt little compunction, under the circumstances, about raiding him or his."[1]

How much politics motivated all the James-Younger gang's crimes has stirred some historical debate. T. J. Stiles writes in his biography of Jesse James that the outlaw's reign of robbery and terror was part of a calculated effort to restore Confederate power in the defeated South. Other historians downplay politics and see a thug who, like many thugs before and since, let greed and a thirst for public attention fuel his deeds. Minnesota may have been targeted in 1876 because the heat from law enforcement was too intense for them back at their home base of Missouri. And as in many criminal tales, the Northfield heist might have been the mythical "last big score"; Cole Younger said the proceeds would let the gang "start life anew in Cuba, South America, or Australia."[2]

The Northfield Raid in particular plays a significant part in the James' saga, since it marked the end of the gang—though not the end of Jesse's crimes. And in an odd twist, there is no direct evidence that the James brothers even took part! In his accounts of the crime, Cole Younger never mentions either by name, and the brothers never admitted they were there. But the detailed historical retellings of the crime place the James brothers in Minnesota in the days leading up to the crime, and few doubt their role in the Northfield Raid.

Jesse James

NOT ACCORDING TO PLAN

The gang began arriving in Minneapolis around August 23, 1876. Some checked into the Nicollet Hotel under assumed names, and there are reports of Jesse visiting a local bordello. Two others stayed at the Merchant's Hotel in St. Paul. Over the next days, the gang hatched its plan, counting on the knowledge of their one Minnesotan, Bill Chadwell, to help them navigate their routes. Within a few days, the eight-member gang split into two groups and began heading out to scout the area around Northfield. Talking to a local farmer just outside the targeted town, one of the gang commented, "Why, according to your statement of the Northfield people, a very few men so inclined could capture the town."[3] The farmer agreed, perhaps giving the hardened robbers an even greater sense of confidence than usual.

The Minnesota Connection

The man usually called Bill Chadwell in the recounting of the Northfield Raid was actually William Stiles. Although a Minnesotan, the sources disagree on whether he was born in Monticello or moved to the state from Missouri. Stiles seems to have had brushes with the law in Minnesota before adopting his alias and hooking up with the James-Younger gang. He also apparently still had relatives in the state at the time of the raid. A wrinkle in the Chadwell-Stiles story came in 1931, when a man calling himself Bill Stiles said he had taken part in the robbery, along with a man called Bill Chadwell. But most historians accept that Stiles and Chadwell are one and the same, and that he met his end in the streets of Northfield.

By September 6, Cole Younger's group was in Millersburg, 11 miles west of Northfield, while the rest of the gang was at Cannon City. The next day, they rendezvoused in Northfield. The plan was to send three men into the bank first, most likely the James brothers and Charlie Pitts, with Younger and Clell Miller to follow. The other three would stay at a nearby bridge. The men outside the bank were to keep the streets clear and scare off any would-be heroes while the others carried out the robbery.

From the start, however, the plan went awry. The three men assigned to go inside went in too early, before Cole and Miller reached the bank door to stand guard. When they did reach their position, local hardware store owner J. S. Allen was about to go inside. After Miller ordered him to turn around, Allen took off, shouting, "Get your guns, boys, they're robbing the bank."[4] The townspeople would heed the call.

Meanwhile, inside the bank, things were also deviating from the plan. The robbers had entered with their usual bravado, shouting their intention to rob the bank and warning everyone inside, "If you hallo we will blow your God-damned brains out."[5] When learning the head cashier wasn't there to open the safe, the gang turned to assistant cashier Joseph Heywood. But as Heywood explained, the safe was on a time lock and he couldn't open it. Seeing that the door to the vault was open, one of the bandits entered it. Heywood quickly shut the door, trapping him inside—and unleashing the fury of the remaining two robbers.

Heywood soon felt cold steel on his neck, the blade of a knife one of the robbers wielded. "Open that door or we'll cut you from car to car," the bandit said.[6] Heywood, a seasoned Civil War vet himself, broke free, but soon absorbed the blow of a revolver crashing against his head. The robbers continued to demand money, and one fired his gun. In the ongoing confusion, bank teller Alonzo Bunker tried to make a break for the door and was shot in the shoulder for his attempted escape. Wounded, he managed to get outside, where more mayhem was unfolding.

THE GANG TAKES FLIGHT

At almost the same time the first bullet was fired inside the bank, Cole Younger set off a warning shot, to alert the gang members back at the bridge that the robbery was going wrong. Jim Younger and his cohorts at the bridge quickly reached the bank, firing their guns and telling the townspeople to go back inside their homes. But the people of Northfield were not about to let

Six members of the James-Younger gang; the Younger brothers are 4, 5 and 6

anyone, even the Cole-Younger gang, disrupt life in their town without a fight. Resident Elias Stacy had arrived on the scene with a shotgun, and its blast caught Clell Miller in the face. Manning, the hardware store owner, killed one of the robbers' horses. A second shot from his gun hit Cole Younger in the thigh; a third proved fatal to Bill Chadwell, piercing his heart. Meanwhile, a bullet from medical student Henry Wheeler's gun finished off Miller, while another wounded Bob Younger.

The men inside the bank finally came out, but not before one of them killed assistant cashier Heywood. T. J. Stiles speculates it was Jesse James who pulled the trigger, while Cole Younger later claimed it was Charlie Pitts. No one knows for sure. Whoever killed him, a newspaper reported that Heywood was left "with his brain and blood oozing slowly from his right temple."[7] Outside, along with the two dead robbers, was Nicholas Gustavson, a bystander who was hit in the shootout and would soon die from his wound.

As Northfield residents surveyed the scene around the bank, the six remaining gang members began their flight. They had no time to destroy the local telegraph office, so news of the attempted robbery and their escape spread quickly. So did the offer of a reward from Minnesota governor John S. Pillsbury: $1,000 for each man, dead or alive.

At first the gang managed to outrun the news of their crime, passing through Dundas and Millersburg unchallenged. Outside Shieldsville, though, they exchanged shots with local residents who realized who they were. As the gang moved on, they reached unfamiliar territory. As Cole Younger wrote, "When we got into the big woods and among the lakes we were practically lost."[8] They moved slowly at times, stopping to treat Bob Younger's shattered elbow, and abandoning their horses since the posse would be looking for men on horseback. They trudged on through the rain, at one point encountering a man named Dunning. Some of the gang wanted to kill him. Instead they let him go after making him promise not to tell authorities the gang's whereabouts. Dunning agreed, but then almost immediately broke his promise when he reached Mankato.

Still eluding capture after a week on the run, the gang decided to split up. Cole Younger, in his account, says Howard and Woods left the other four. T. J. Stiles says it was Frank and Jesse James who separated from the gang, stealing horses and beginning their getaway to the Dakota Territory. They sometimes went by the aliases of Howard and Woodson. Along the way, both men were wounded by buckshot, but they managed to escape capture.

Cole Younger had directed the others to Madelia, where he thought they could get horses. Cole, who had stayed in the town before the heist, was spotted by a resident who recognized him, and soon another posse was after them. The posse cut them off from reaching the horses and the four robbers retreated into some bushes. Hearing a small contingent of the posse preparing to attack, the Younger brothers and Charlie Pitts readied for a charge of their own. As bullets flew, Pitts fell dead, shot through the heart. Each Younger was wounded, and Bob called out, "I surrender. They're all down but me . . . I'll not shoot."[9] Sheriff James Glispin ordered his men to stand down, and later assured Younger that the posse would protect them from a rumored lynch mob. "But the only mob that came," Younger wrote, "was the mob of sightseers, reporters, and detectives."[10]

Memories of the Younger Gang

The Minnesota Historical Society has a bystander's account of the arrest of the Younger Brothers, reflecting the memories of Charles Armstrong. He was nine years old when he saw the outlaws brought into Madelia.

"The armed posse stood around the wagon. As the wagon started towards the town ¼ mile from the station, boy like I followed [sic]. Jim Younger who had been shot in the chin and was bleeding badly, had his face over the wagon side. When we passed one house, a woman hurried to the wagon and gave him a white handkerchief, which he held to his chin . . . The body of Charlie Pitts was in the very small jail and the door open so any who chose could go in and see the body, which we did."[11]

TRIAL AND PRISON

In jail in Madelia, the Youngers had a string of visitors: reporters, Christian women seeking to save their souls, people bearing gifts of food and cigars. At one point, Cole Younger blamed his life of crime on his military service, and explained the Northfield robbery as revenge on the state for gambling losses the gang had suffered in St. Paul.

The trio was moved to the jail at Faribault, and in November 1876, the Younger brothers were formally indicted on four counts: the murders of Heywood and Gustavson, the assault on Bunker, and the robbery itself. Cole Younger maintained that he and his brothers had killed no one. Their lawyers said that as accessories to the crimes, they could face the death penalty, unless they pleaded guilty. The Youngers took their lawyers' advice and each was sentenced to life at Stillwater State Prison.

Bob Younger served almost 13 years at Stillwater, dying there in 1889. His brothers, both before and after his death, held a variety of jobs. For a time, Cole was the prison librarian, and for about a decade was the head nurse at the hospital. Cole reported that the doctors he met were "staunch partisans . . . in the efforts of our friends to secure our pardons."[12]

Cole and James Younger are paroled in 1901

The efforts of others inside and outside the prison won Jim and Cole Younger their release in 1901. Soon after his release, Cole Younger told a reporter he had "reached the limit of my capacity for taking punishment."[13] But unlike Jesse James, at least he had survived his punishment. Jesse had been shot dead in 1882. Frank meanwhile, teamed up with his old partner Cole for a legitimate pursuit. In 1903 they launched a show called "The Great Cole Younger and Frank James Historical Wild West."

The Murder of Kitty Ging

THE CRIME: A supposed lover arranges the murder of his girlfriend to collect on life insurance policies

PERPETRATORS: Harry Hayward, with the help of Claus Blixt

VICTIM: Catherine "Kitty" Ging

SCENE OF THE CRIME: In a carriage on the streets of Minneapolis

WHEN: December 3, 1894

Ozark Flats

Greed motivates people to commit crimes and violate trust. And greed may have also led Catherine "Kitty" Ging to her death. Of course meeting the charming but diabolical Harry Hayward—who may or may not have been a serial killer—didn't help either.

A lust for money, ill-gotten if need be, seemed to drive Hayward during his brief 30 years. His father owned and operated an apartment building known as the Ozark Flats on Hennepin Avenue in Minneapolis. (Later transformed into the Bellevue Hotel, the building is still standing and now houses condos.) The young Haywood occasionally helped out with the family business, but his real "job" was gambling. He had his first taste of the financial and emotional thrill of winning at a gambling establishment on Nicollet Avenue. Starting on the roulette wheel, he moved to the faro table, sometimes wagering $1,000 on one bet. At times, he won large amounts of money. Like most serious gamblers, he lost more often. But that didn't stop him from finding another stake and placing down another bet. As he said several times in the last weeks of his life, "Money is my God!"[1]

MEETING KITTY

Despite his seedy occupation, Hayward traveled in well-heeled Minneapolis social circles, and his good looks and intelligence gave him a way with the ladies. One of the woman he charmed was Kitty Ging, a seamstress. A native New Yorker, she had done well in her chosen career after settling in the Twin Cities. She met Hayward in January 1894, and the two soon discovered their shared love of wealth. Ging gave Hayward money to gamble, which he lost, yet the two deepened their relationship as they discussed the gambler's plans to buy stolen jewels and sell them. And Ging passed counterfeit money that Hayward gave her. Nothing seemed to shock the young woman about her new beau, even if they didn't see eye to eye about the nature of their relationship. Hayward supposedly told others they were going to get married. Ging, who had broken off an earlier engagement, didn't seem to share the sentiment, as she was sometimes seen with other men.

Even if marriage was not in the cards, Hayward had enough sway over his girlfriend to win her trust more than once. The last episode came in November 1894 when he convinced her to take out two life insurance policies worth a total of $10,000 and name Hayward as the beneficiary. Around this time, Ging took an apartment at the Ozark Flats, along with her niece Louise.

Several months before these events, Hayward had already begun setting the trap for his supposed fiancée. He began looking for an accomplice, someone who would actually do the murderous deed. He asked his brother Adry if he could kill someone for a fee. Adry was not particularly strong willed; some later hinted he had

A contemporary account of the case against Hayward

mental problems. But he also lacked his brother's sociopathic tendencies and told Harry he would not kill anyone.

Hayward then turned to Claus Blixt, a Swedish immigrant who worked as a handyman and janitor for Hayward's father at the Ozark Flats. As Hayward later said—almost bragged—before his execution, he "hypnotized" Blixt with the lure of money. In their conversations, Hayward also talked casually about murder, that killing a person was little different from killing a rat or a mouse. With the offer of money and a little flattery, Hayward found his hired killer.

Adry Hayward, not sure what to make of his brother's intentions, approached a family friend on November 30 and told him he thought Harry might be concocting a murder scheme. The friend scoffed. But just several days later, a murder took place in Minneapolis. With the death of Kitty Ging, it was hard to dismiss Adry's claim.

THE KILLING

On the evening of December 3, 1894, Kitty Ging was at the West Hotel. She called for a carriage, drawn by a horse she had used before, and headed off for a 7:30 p.m. appointment with Harry Hayward. He had told her he had a business idea he wanted to discuss. But before that, he met with Claus Blixt.

At the Ozark Flats, around 6:30 p.m., Hayward told the janitor that tonight was the night—the night he would kill Ging. A nervous Blixt tried to back out of the deal; Hayward threatened to kill him and his wife if he failed to carry out the plan. "He fixed me with his eyes." Blixt later said, "I couldn't say no when he looked at me that way—nobody could."[2]

Haywood plied the reluctant Blixt with booze then took him to the spot where he was supposed to meet with Ging. The would-be assassin climbed into the carriage as Hayward explained a change in the plans: Blixt and Kitty should take the carriage and meet Hayward at another spot. Ging didn't understand the new plan. Hayward simply said, "Don't ask any questions."[3] The carriage took off, and Hayward hurried to a prearranged opera date—his alibi for the murder.

Blixt and Ging rode for about 15 minutes, mostly in silence, as the janitor tried to work up the courage to commit the crime. Finally, he put a revolver to the young woman's head and pulled the trigger once. Ging fell back. An autopsy would later reveal that the single bullet severed her carotid artery, killing her instantly. Blixt drove the carriage for another mile before dumping her body on Excelsior Boulevard, where it was soon found by a passerby. Blixt then returned to the Ozark Flats.

By the time Blixt reached the building and cleaned the murder weapon, as Hayward had instructed, news had already spread: Something had happened to Kitty Ging. Over the next several days, the police questioned Blixt and the two Hayward brothers, but none of them said a word. Adry's earlier ill feelings, however, had set in motion the legal trap that would snare his brother. After the family friend heard about the murder, he contacted law officials. Adry was arrested and confessed everything he knew about his brother's orchestration of the crime.

FACING JUSTICE

Before the confessions, Harry Hayward had tried to divert any suspicion from himself. He went to see Ging's body in the morgue. Playing the distraught boyfriend, he rubbed her hair and patted her cheek. In his head, he tried to plan out what to do and say next. Finally he blurted out, "You folks think I am guilty, but God knows I am not."[4] Hayward counted on his alibi, and the reticence of Blixt and Adry, to protect him.

But with the process set in motion by Adry several days before, the gambler was not safe. After several days of stonewalling to the police, Blixt confessed to his role in the murder, implicating Hayward as well. The two were indicted on December 13, 1894. In jail, an attorney and old friend, W. E. Hale, came to represent Hayward. Unlike his story to the police and his later testimony in court, Hayward came clean about his role in the killing, stunning Hale, who then refused to represent him. Meanwhile, outside the jail, rumors spread around Minneapolis that if the citizens ever got their hands on Hayward, they would lynch him—a notion that seemed to scare Hayward more than confronting his legal fate.

The murder had brought national attention to Minneapolis, and as Hayward's trial began early the next year, reporters from San Francisco to New York covered the event. While he was under arrest, Hayward showed a bravado that impressed some, even the jailers who knew all criminal types. No one knew how much he feared the threat of mob justice.

The trial began on January 21, 1895. The key witnesses for the prosecution were Blixt and Adry Hayward. When the Hayward brother took the stand, the defense attorneys objected, saying Adry was insane. The judge retorted, "I don't see that he's any more insane than some of the attorneys in this case."[5] Adry then recounted several conversations with his brother, including one in which he asked Harry, "You're not going to kill the dressmaker, are you?" Harry replied, "Yes, we are."[6]

Later in the day, amidst the scene of one brother helping to condemn another to death, their mother spoke out. "How could you do it?" Mrs. Hayward demanded of her youngest son. Adry held his mother and said, "I had to, mother, it was my duty."[7]

When Hayward took the stand, he lied about everything that happened the night of December 3 and suggested that Adry was the one always in need of money and so had a motive for the murder. The defense also tried to suggest that some unknown "third man" had arranged Ging's killing. But the jury didn't buy any of it. When testimony ended in March, the jurors needed less than three hours—including time for lunch—to find Hayward guilty. The court sentenced him to execution by hanging.

The Ozark Flats building

THE LAST DAYS OF HARRY HAYWARD

Hayward's defense won a stay of execution while it appealed the verdict to the Minnesota Supreme Court. The higher court, however, refused to over-turn it, and Hayward was sentenced to die on December 11, 1895. Even while in jail, Hayward could not stop plotting, asking one visitor to arrange for the beating of one of Hayward's perceived enemies on the outside. The visitor demurred. Another visitor before the execution was Adry Hayward, whose appearance spurred Harry into what one observer called "a demonic rage."[8] But when Adry returned right before the execution, the two brothers reconciled.

By that time, Harry had begun a lengthy and fascinating confession, which went far beyond the killing of Kitty Ging. He described a life of murder and mayhem that had begun years before. Most news reports, however, focused on the public confession he later made right before his death.

On the morning of December 11, Harry Hayward was led to the gallows. The *Minneapolis Tribune* reported that "with a firm step the prisoner went up the platform to meet his last hour."[9] Hayward, in his last statement, said "Some of you think I am a regular devil, and I have no doubt, if you knew my whole past life, you would be firmly convinced of that fact."[10] Then, he confessed to the murder of Kitty Ging. A few moments later, the hangman did his duty.

What About Blixt?

The trial of Claus Blixt was delayed until after Harry Hayward's. Having already confessed to his role in the murder, Blixt pleaded guilty and was sentenced to life in prison. He entered Stillwater State Prison on May 6, 1895, and served thirty years, dying there at the age of 72.

The murder was front-page news for weeks

SERIAL KILLER?

The case of Harry Hayward and Kitty Ging has fascinated true-crime buffs for years—including Minnesotan Jack El-Hai. In 2010, he suggested that Hayward was a serial killer. The evidence came from the jail confession he gave to his cousin Edward Goodsell and several other men. Goodsell published it privately in 1896, along with his own observations of his convicted cousin. The book was not widely available until it was digitized and put on the Internet, where El-Hai found it. The complete confession may not portray Hayward as a "regular devil," but it does describe three other killings Hayward claimed to have committed before December 1894, along with other crimes. Adry Hayward, on the witness stand, also said that his brother told him of three previous murders.

Was Harry Hayward telling the truth as his death approached? El Hai contacted a criminal expert who said most deathbed confessions are real. No one other than Hayward knows for sure if he committed those other murders. But the killing of Kitty Ging was definitely his last.

ANOTHER NOTABLE MINNESOTA CRIME

WARTIME PATRIOTISM

By the time the United States entered World War I in 1917, Minnesota had a sizable German immigrant population. As in other German-American communities across the country, some were not eager for the United States to fight their homeland. To patriotic Americans who supported the war, the hesitancy of the Germans led to questions about their loyalty—and in John Meints's case, to violence. On the night of August 19, 1918, a group of men from Luverne forced Meints from his home, tarred and feathered him, then dumped him over the South Dakota border. The men were charged with several crimes, including kidnapping, but were acquitted, which prompted celebrations in the streets of Luverne. Meints appealed and a new trial resulted in his winning a $6,000 settlement.

A photo of Meints after the attack

Family Matters

Louise Arbogast

THE CRIME: A butcher is brutally murdered in his home, and his family tries to keep it quiet

PERPETRATORS: Mina Arbogast is tried and acquitted; Louise Arbogast is also a possible suspect

VICTIM: Louis Arbogast

SCENE OF THE CRIME: St. Paul

WHEN: May 13, 1909

Butchering proved to be a lucrative career for Louis Arbogast, who set up shop in the Seven Corners neighborhood and owned a large Italianate house nearby. In 1909, Arbogast lived there with his wife Mina and four of their five daughters, a fine example of middle-class respectability. If there were a black sheep in the family or a blot on the Arbogast name, it might have been Louise, Arbogast's oldest girl. At 23, she still lived at home. Louise had struggled with what the local papers later called "nervous ailments," which sent her out of state several times seeking treatment.[1] And it was Louise who drew public attention after the spectacular slaying of her father, one the *Pioneer Press* called the "greatest and most mysterious of the murders which have ever been committed in St. Paul."[2]

A SHOCKING SCENE

Around 4 a.m. on May 13, a streetcar watchman made his rounds near the Arbogast home, when shrieks caught his attention. Others heard the frenzied shouting coming from the Arbogasts', and soon police and neighbors were on the scene. What they found was the naked body of Louis Arbogast sprawled across his bed, which was in flames. His skull had been shattered—with an axe, it was later learned—and feathers covered his body. The smell of gas filled the room and explained the burning bed. Arbogast was alive, barely, when the first people reached the scene, but he died on the way to the hospital. Meanwhile, several half-dressed Arbogast daughters ran screaming through the house and into the street.

The next day, one of Arbogast's employees came to the house when the proprietor didn't show up for work. He was met at the door by a hysterical Louise, who said, "Papa is dead and there is something wrong with the gas."[3] The employee assumed that the young woman meant her father had committed suicide; he was surprised when he later learned that Louis Arbogast had been murdered.

Mina Arbogast and her daughters were decidedly tightlipped in the days after the killing, keeping away reporters and refusing to make any detailed public statements. One comment that did appear, made by 22-year-old Ida Arbogast, was far from complete, merely saying that there was a fire and her father was unconscious when she entered her parents' bedroom. Mrs. Arbogast was reticent with the police as well, as she "skillfully evaded their most cleverly worded questions."[4] But one news report suggested that the family had quarreled the night of the murder, as Louis announced his plans to travel to the Klondike, despite his family's objections.

The consensus among the public soon emerged that someone in the household had committed the crime, perhaps one of the daughters, and Mrs. Arbogast was doing her best to protect the culprit. Most suspicion focused on Louise, given her history of emotional troubles and her behavior after the murder. Her hysteria was so severe that she was hospitalized.

ARREST AND TRIAL

St. Paul police placed members of the Arbogast household under surveillance, and comments exchanged between Louise and her mother led to an arrest. Mina Arbogast had joined her daughter at the hospital and said, "It's between you and me, Louise, and God knows I did not kill your father."[5] Louise then denied she had done it, adding an odd comment about the spirit of her father coming down to protect her mother.

Those comments and Louise's history led police to arrest her on May 17. Under questioning by authorities, Louise denied she had killed her father, that she was insane, as many claimed, and also denied that her mother had committed the crime. Despite that assertion, both Louise and her mother were indicted for first-degree murder. Louise surprised some by waiving her right to a hearing that would determine if she were insane.

Louise Arbogast, who was accused of her father's murder

The first trial was delayed until October. During the ensuing months, hints of motives for the killing were discussed in the press: Louis wanted Louise to take the trip to the Klondike with him, and someone in the family didn't want her to go. Louise was her father's favorite, and perhaps someone else in the family was jealous of the trip or other favoritism he seemed to show.

Anyone hoping to have these questions cleared up during the trial was disappointed. Mina Arbogast was tried first, with each of her daughters testifying. They seemed hazy on the details of the events of May 12–13, and at times other witnesses contradicted their accounts. A neighbor's testimony disputed Ida's account of her mother's whereabouts when the fire was discovered; Ida claimed Mina had been in the burning bed when she entered her parents' room. The neighbor, though, said Mina had been in the kitchen. Hearing the testimony, Ida "squirmed in her chair and the agonized expression of her face betrayed her feelings."[6]

As the jury deliberated, they asked the court if they could find Mrs. Arbogast guilty of a lesser charge. The judge said no—either she was guilty of first-degree murder or she must be acquitted. The jury voted for acquittal. The *Pioneer Press* editorialized about the police's ineptitude while investigating the case, and prosecutors dropped the charges against Louise Arbogast. St. Paul police, meanwhile, believed they had arrested the murderer, even if no one was convicted.

The unsolved murder of Louis Arbogast has led to much speculation about what went on behind closed doors in his fancy home. Most assume that one of the women of his family was guilty, but who it was, and why she murdered Louis, remains a mystery.

The Wife Gets It

THE CRIME: A husband hires out-of-state killers to murder his wife

PERPETRATORS: Frank Dunn, killers Joseph Redenbaugh and Frank McCool

VICTIM: Alice McQuillan

SCENE OF THE CRIME: St. Paul

WHEN: April 26, 1917

Joseph Redenbaugh

Alice McQuillan was a pretty 24-year-old when she began her whirlwind May-December romance with Frank Dunn. Despite their 16-year age difference, Alice and Frank at least shared some social standing; her father owned a successful plumbing company, and Frank made good money off a government contract transporting mail. Their brief romance led to a quick wedding and a honeymoon in Duluth. The relationship, though, soured quickly, and Frank's true feelings for his young bride would emerge three years later.

A QUICK SEPARATION

The couple moved into a house Dunn owned on Smith Avenue in St. Paul. It only took several months of matrimony for Dunn to learn that his new wife tended to be nervous and sickly. In turn, whether by nature or as a reaction to his wife, Dunn showed himself to be an impatient man with a bad temper. After just a few months together, Alice left for her parents' home, but the McQuillans convinced her to give the marriage another try. She did, but then Frank left, moving to the house he owned next door.

In June 1915, Alice took legal steps against her husband, obtaining a separation on the grounds of cruelty. The court demanded that Frank pay her $70 a month, a decision which seemed to upset him. The McQuillans, in turn had no respect for Frank Dunn. He would later say he had no enemies in the world, "except my wife's people."[1]

With the separation in place, the estranged couple went their own ways, though for a time both lived in the West. Then in April 1917, they were both back in St. Paul. Frank sent Alice an Easter card; she called him to see about getting together, and they met at a local drugstore. The conversation went well, with Frank seemingly remorseful about how things had turned out. They talked about a reconciliation and setting up a new home in Minneapolis.

MURDER FOR HIRE

Dunn's words, though, and the tears he shed as he met with Alice, were all a ruse. The anger he had felt back in 1915 after the separation had not dissipated. Back then, Dunn had talked to two Montana hoodlums about the possibility of murdering Alice. He promised them $10,000 for the deed. Dunn, though, learned the risk of entering the underworld; the two men said they would go to the police and squeal on Dunn if he didn't pay them. Needless to say, they weren't interested in committing the murder. The blackmail cost Dunn a little over $5,000.

In April 1917, with Alice back in St. Paul, Dunn's thoughts once again turned to murder. This time he used a local bartender named Mike Moore as a go-between. Moore, something of a criminal fixer, arranged for two Kansas City thugs to carry out Dunn's murder-for-hire.

One of them was Joe Redenbaugh, a slight, pimply teen who had already spent plenty of time in reformatories. The other was Frank McCool. The two men arrived in the Twin Cites area on April 24. Before they could carry out their mission, though, they got tangled in another crime that eventually led to their undoing, along with Moore's and Dunn's.

JOSEPH REDENBAUGH AND HIS GIRL BRIDE, PEARL HEITKAMP REDENBAUGH, who were arrested in San Francisco charged with the murder of Mrs. Alice Quiller Dunn in St. Paul last April.

Joseph Redenbaugh and his wife, Pearl

Redenbaugh and McCool were stopped for speeding by Minneapolis officer George Connery. They had no money to pay a fine, so the two men kidnapped the officer, took him to Anoka County, shot him in the leg, then beat him to death. The two killers then headed back to the Twin Cities. They had another murder to commit.

The night of April 25, Frank Dunn went to a local club, then made sure his housekeeper saw him return home. With his alibi in place, all Dunn could do was wait and see if everything went according to plan. It did.

Around 1:30 a.m., McCool and Redenbaugh entered the McQuillan home. Redenbaugh went upstairs and found Alice sharing a bed with her younger sister Katherine. Something woke up Katherine, who called to her sister as she saw Redenbaugh, his face covered with a mask, approaching the bed. Redenbaugh tried to quiet Katherine with these less-than-soothing words: "Be quiet, be calm. I am only going to do a little shooting."[2] With that, the murderer took out his gun and shot Alice three times.

MANHUNT

St. Paul police, under the direction of the notorious chief John J. O'Connor, arrested Dunn, though they did not charge him with murder. Soon, though, information came out about his earlier attempt to hire two hit men to kill his wife.

McCool's confession implicates Redenbaugh

Then, using fingerprints found at the scene, the police identified Redenbaugh as Alice's killer. As a manhunt went on, Officer Connery's body was discovered. Both he and Alice McQuillan had been killed by a .44 caliber gun, and Chief O'Connor thought the two murders were linked.

On May 8, McCool was arrested in Nebraska, wanted as a suspect in a robbery there. He still carried the .44 caliber gun he and Redenbaugh had taken from the Minneapolis officer and used in both shootings. The St. Paul police had already received a tip that the two criminals had been in the Twin Cites around April 26. Then, on May 11, police arrested Redenbaugh and his new bride. Returned to Minnesota, Redenbaugh confessed to his role in the two killings in order to spare his wife from being implicated in the crimes. Redenbaugh also said that Frank Dunn was the mastermind of the McQuillan murder. McCool, too, came clean about his role in the case. Soon Dunn, bartender Moore, and a third accomplice to the murder were all indicted.

With his confession, Redenbaugh received a life sentence for the Connery killing and a lesser term for the murder of Alice Dunn. McCool was sentenced to thirty years for killing Connery. The trial of Frank Dunn was the legal highlight of the case, and women from the Twin Cities waited in line to enter the courthouse. With the words of the men he hired in 1915 and again in 1917 damning him, Dunn was convicted of first-degree murder. He received a life sentence and died in jail. Redenbaugh, though, found redemption of a sort in prison. A 1957 article in *The Atlantic* highlighted his case to argue against the death penalty. Redenbaugh, the author wrote, "accomplished a remarkable job of self-reform or cure. He grew from an unmoral, undisciplined, semiliterate 'tramp kid' into a peaceable, law-abiding, highly educated man."[3] He was eventually released from prison in 1962.

ANOTHER NOTABLE MINNESOTA CRIME

A BOOTLEGGER'S KIDNAPPING

During Prohibition, Leon Gleckman was one of the underworld figures in the Twin Cities who used bootlegging to build a small criminal empire. In 1931, he was kidnapped by other crime figures. Gleckman's ransom was reduced several times, until he was finally freed for just $5,000. Well-known crime fixer Jack Peifer got credit for winning Gleckman's release. But what wasn't known until later was that he had also arranged the snatching in the first place. Gleckman had once hijacked liquor that was Peifer's, creating bad blood between them. Gleckman, thankful for his quick and safe release, publicly praised the St. Paul police force, which provided guards around his house.

The Circus Lynchings

The jail cell that the mob broke into

Minnesota Historical Society

THE CRIME: A mob lynches three African Americans accused of raping a white woman

PERPETRATORS: Henry Stephenson, the alleged leader of the mob; various white Duluth residents indicted for rioting, inciting a riot, or murder

VICTIMS: Isaac McGhie, Elmer Jackson, and Elias Clayton

SCENE OF THE CRIME: Second Avenue East and First Street, Duluth

WHEN: June 15, 1920

For decades, the arrival of a circus in an American town was a much-anticipated event. P.T. Barnum and his business associates set the standard in the late 1800s, and the Ringling Brothers carried on the tradition before and after their merger with Barnum's enterprise. But other circuses also traveled the country, bringing plenty of entertainment—and perhaps a sense of mystery, given the itinerant lifestyle and closed cultural community of the circus workers. When John Robinson's Circus rolled into Duluth in 1920, it sparked one of the most heinous crimes in Minnesota history.

A NIGHT AT THE CIRCUS

The Robinson circus pitched its tents for two performances on June 14. The troupe billed itself as "the finest in the world," promising "herds of performing elephants" and "droves of camels."[1] The lineup also included acrobats and aerialists. In all, some 1,500 people worked at the circus, many of them African-American hands who set up the tents at each stop then quickly took them down when the shows were over.

One of the Duluth residents who braved storm clouds and came out for the evening show on the 14th was 18-year-old Irene Tusken. At the circus, she met her boyfriend, James Sullivan. When the show was over, the couple hung around for a while, watching the crew take down the tents. A little later, Tusken and Sullivan were on a streetcar to the girl's home. After dropping her off, Sullivan headed off to work at the midnight shift at the city's docks.

According to Sullivan's later statements, something terrible happened in between the end of the circus and that streetcar ride home. Some time after midnight, he told his father that six black circus workers had accosted him and Tusken. With a gun to his head and the threat of having his brains splattered on the ground, Sullivan could only watch helplessly as the men sexually assaulted his girlfriend. His father then notified Duluth police chief John Murphy of the alleged crime.

By this time, the Robinson circus was loaded on its train cars and about to head to its next destination. With a small squadron of officers accompanying him, Murphy halted the train before it could leave the Duluth, Winnipeg & Pacific rail yard. The chief and his officers took 13 African-American men off the train, questioned them, and took six to the local jail.

Sullivan's story did not arouse any suspicion due to the racist atmosphere of the time, and possibly because of a bias against circus workers. The angry officers threw around the word *nigger* as they confronted the alleged assailants. But Sullivan could not identify any of the six he claimed raped Tusken. And the young girl, after getting home from the circus, said nothing to her parents about the brutal assault that supposedly took place. The next day, a doctor's examination showed no signs of rape or other violence.

A MOB ENRAGED

The local paper seemed ready to believe Sullivan's allegations. A headline on the June 15 *Duluth Herald* read, "West Duluth Girl Victim of Six Negroes." It also reported that three of the arrested men had confessed to taking part in the crime, after being "sweated" by police. The article went on to describe how Tusken was "in a hysterical condition and very weak" after the alleged assault.[2] To a private detective, Tusken said she had blacked out after four of the men grabbed her. When she regained consciousness, only her arms were a little sore. Asked why she didn't tell anyone about the attack right afterward, the victim replied, "I thought it best to keep quiet."[3]

The *Herald* was an evening paper, and even before it laid out the story of the assault, rumors had spread around West Duluth about what happened after the circus ended. Angry men drove through the streets on the back of a truck, inciting anger against the alleged attackers. They encouraged others to join the "necktie party" they planned to throw at the city jail.

By 9 p.m., as many as 10,000 people were outside the jail, demanding their version of "justice." Convinced of the black men's guilt, they thought they deserved death for the rape of a white woman. And since the death penalty had been abolished in Minnesota almost a decade before, the mob felt it would have to take the law into its own hands to deliver what it considered an appropriate punishment.

Abolishing the Death Penalty

The state of Minnesota had executed convicted killers for almost 50 years when William Williams went to the gallows in 1906. Found guilty of killing a boy he knew and the boy's mother, Williams had said he had been drinking and didn't know what happened, but his guilt seemed clear. His execution, though, was botched when the hangman used a rope that was too long. Three law officials had to grab the rope and lift Williams off the floor for almost 15 minutes, until he finally died. The execution-gone-awry fueled efforts that had already been building in the state to abolish capital punishment. Some abolitionists opposed the spectacle of the executions. Others condemned the cruel nature of the punishment. In 1911, with backing from Governor Adolph Eberhart, the state legislature outlawed the death penalty.

The jail cell the angry mob broke into to snatch the lynching victims

Wielding a variety of makeshift weapons, including bricks and timbers, the surging mob stormed the jail, smashing windows and tearing down doors. A district judge tried to pacify the crowd, reminding it of the disgrace that had recently befallen Omaha, Nebraska, after racial violence there. The mob, though, would not be appeased. And the waves of anger intensified after a false rumor spread along the street that Irene Tusken was on her deathbed, if not dead already.

The outnumbered police in the station tried to hold off the mob, at one point using a fire hose to try to push it back. The relentless men leading the attack managed to commandeer the hose and turn it on the officers. Soon several hundred members of the mob were inside the police station, deaf to pleas to let the legal system take its course with the six accused men. "We don't care if they're guilty or innocent," someone shouted. "Kill the black snakes!"[4]

THE LYNCHINGS

A contingent of the mob approached the cell where the six African Americans feared for their lives. They watched as local resident Harry Stephenson swung a sledgehammer against the iron bars that stood between them and the mob. Others in the crowd brandished a railroad iron to break into the cell. The mob grabbed three men from this cell and another nearby, then dragged them outside.

The lynching was front-page news nationwide

The unfortunate trio was Isaac McGhie, Elmer Jackson and Elias Clayton. McGhie and Clayton had been beaten, and McGhie had tearfully proclaimed his innocence to the uncaring mob. A white wave of bodies pushed the three men along Superior Street, with some people trying to kick the three helpless blacks. The crowd directed the three to a light pole, where their "sentence" would be carried out.

A Catholic priest emerged from the crowd and tried to stop the lynching. As the *Associated Press* reported, "Father W. J. Powers made a plea for the lives of the Negroes. Father Powers climbed the pole already selected by the mob and asked for law and order and was met by 'to hell with law.'"[5] Then Isaac McGhie found himself with a rope around his neck. Still professing his innocence, his body was lifted off the ground. By one report, the rope broke, then another, before one strong enough was found. Elmer Jackson was next to die, then Elias Clayton. The crowd ignored the pleas to spare his life. Amidst the brutal killings, the press reported, bystanders laughed. One man "mounted a pole above a dying Negro and kicked him repeatedly in the face."[6] When the three were dead, members of the crowd posed around the pole for a photograph with the lifeless bodies.

SEEKING JUSTICE

According to one news report, the Duluth vigilante killings were the first lynchings in Minnesota in 20 years. Blacks were a tiny part of the state's population in 1920—fewer than 9,000 in a state of almost 2.4 million. But one historian speculates that the arrival of some African Americans in Duluth to work at the local steel plant—at lower wages than whites received—stirred some racial animosity. The *Minneapolis Tribune* at the time asserted that the alleged assailants' color was the spark of the violence, an explanation the St. Paul branch of the National Association for the Advancement of Colored People (NAACP) also accepted.

The NAACP took an interest in the lynchings from the start, demanding the removal of the dangling dead bodies of McGhie, Jackson and Clayton. The president of the St. Paul branch also happened to be Minnesota governor J. A. A. Burnquist, who sent National Guard troops to Duluth to restore order. They found a mostly quiet city, with the mob dispersed. Now, the case would turn to the courts, as the NAACP and others sought to arrest, try and convict the men who led the lynchings. Some civic groups in Duluth also demanded that the perpetrators face up to their crime. At the same time, the NAACP wanted to defend other black circus workers still being held. Another group of men had been brought to Duluth after Chief Murphy hauled in the initial six.

As the legal proceedings unfolded, news of the lynchings spread, drawing reactions from several national papers. *The New York Times* noted that lynchings were obviously not confined to the South, and that officials in Duluth had trouble getting statements from people who witnessed the event. Meanwhile, before the end of June, at least some Duluthians were beginning to question the story Irene Tusken and Jimmie Sullivan had spun to police back on June 15.

Before the end of the month, a grand jury handed out the first of 37 indictments against men charged with rioting or first-degree murder; some were charged with both. Seven black circus workers were also indicted for rape (an odd number given that three of the supposed rapists were already dead and there were only six in total). Eventually, though, just two of those men stood trial for their charge.

As the summer unfolded, the legal proceeding took two tracks, with the rioters going to court first. Prosecutors managed to bring just eight whites to trial. Only three were convicted, including the sledgehammer-swinging Henry Stephenson, and none for murder. None of the three served more than 15 months in jail.

That fall, the remaining two accused rapists, Max Mason and William Miller, went on trial. The NAACP brought in a top-shelf Chicago lawyer to represent Mason. Ferdinand Lee Barnett, stepson of the famed reformer Ida Barnett, showed the weakness of Tusken's and Sullivan's stories, particularly about how they identified their assailants. He introduced testimony that highlighted the lack of physical evidence that would corroborate a gang rape. He admitted, "Something did happen at the circus grounds"—most likely the two white teens were robbed of some jewelry.[7] But no brutal assault took place.

The Duluth memorial to the three victims

The jury, though, did not buy Barnett's arguments. It found Mason guilty of rape and sentenced him to thirty years in prison. Miller was able to win acquittal, thanks in part to a witness placing him somewhere else at the time of the crime. Mason appealed his verdict to the state Supreme Court and lost. The one dissenting, judge, however found that "the evidence does not sustain the conviction," finding it particularly odd that Irene Tusken could be so seemingly unperturbed in the hours following her alleged rape.[8]

Minnesota lawyer and writer John D. Bessler has written about the stain the lynchings left on the city of Duluth. For decades, many residents preferred to act as if they had never happened. Finally, in 1991, the city marked the graves of Isaac McGhie, Elmer Jackson and Elias Clayton. A decade later, city officials held a Week of Remembrance, to recall the injustice of the past and work for better race relations in the future.

ANOTHER NOTABLE MINNESOTA CRIME

WABASHA STREET CAVES "MASSACRE"

The caves carved into St. Paul's sandstone bluffs overlooking the Mississippi once housed the Castle Royal, an upscale nightclub and gambling hall that catered to the gangsters the came to the city during the '20s and '30s. Legend has it that a gangland massacre also took place in the Castle Royal, as one mobster turned his machine gun on three associates. Supposedly the three victims' bodies were buried under a cement floor in the cave, and holes still in the walls are said to be bullet holes. The cave massacre seems more legend than fact, though some insist more details never emerged because St. Paul police helped cover up the crime. Today, the caves are home to a company that offers tours of some of St. Paul's famous criminal locations—and the gangsters' ghosts are said to haunt their final resting place.

Minnesota Historical Society

Castle Royal in its heyday

When the Criminal Becomes the Victim

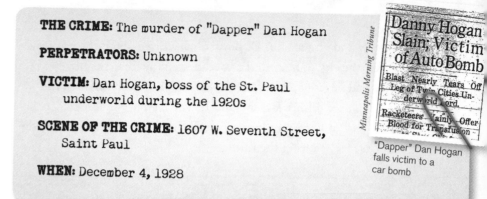

THE CRIME: The murder of "Dapper" Dan Hogan

PERPETRATORS: Unknown

VICTIM: Dan Hogan, boss of the St. Paul underworld during the 1920s

SCENE OF THE CRIME: 1607 W. Seventh Street, Saint Paul

WHEN: December 4, 1928

Minneapolis Morning Tribune

Danny Hogan Slain; Victim of Auto Bomb

Blast Nearly Tears Off Leg of Twin Cities Underworld Lord.

Racketeers Vainly Offer Blood for Transfusion

"Dapper" Dan Hogan falls victim to a car bomb

Many residents of the Twin Cities knew "Dapper" Dan Hogan as the proprietor of the Green Lantern, a bar on North Wabasha Street in St. Paul. Hogan shared the wealth of his business, bringing turkeys to the needy at Christmas time. But whatever its charms as a watering hole, the Green Lantern was hardly the source of the money that paid for Hogan's largesse. Hogan built his fortune by taking advantage of the "O'Connor System," an arrangement set up during the early 1900s between then-St. Paul police chief John O'Connor and gangsters, hoodlums and crooks of all stripes.

The essence of the system was simple: Pay me a bribe and don't commit crimes in my city, O'Connor told criminals, and my officers will leave you alone. With the O'Connor System in place, St. Paul's reputation as a safe haven for crooks spread across the country, and during the Prohibition Era, many of America's most notorious bank robbers, bootleggers and gang leaders spent some time in the city. And at times the crooks themselves took a hand at law enforcement: Petty thieves might receive a talk from more powerful gangsters who didn't want their cozy deal with O'Connor and his successors sabotaged. A reporter from the era later recalled, "It was a safer town to live in for most people when you had the criminals making sure there was no crime."[1]

Minneapolis's Days of Corruption

Before Dan Hogan helped perfect the O'Connor System, the other Twin City had a reputation as a center of criminality as well. Under Mayor A. A. "Doc" Ames, Minneapolis was briefly a hotbed of police corruption, which allowed crooks a free-wheeling lifestyle. First elected in

A. A. "Doc" Ames

1876, Ames was mayor on several different occasions, once switching parties when it suited his political purposes. After his election in 1900, he named his brother chief of police, and set up a system that let all sorts of criminal activity flourish—for a price. Muckraking journalist Lincoln Steffens profiled Ames and his corrupt reign in 1903. He wrote that Ames's ways "did not arouse the citizens, but it did attract criminals, and more and more thieves and swindlers came hurrying to Minneapolis. Some of them saw the police, and made terms. Some were seen by the police and invited to go to work. There was room for all. This astonishing fact that the government of a city asked criminals to rob the people is fully established."[2] By the time Steffens's article "The Shame of Minneapolis" appeared, Ames was gone as mayor, having resigned several months before. The baton of police graft would pass to St. Paul.

HOGAN AND THE SYSTEM

Behind the façade of respectability Dan Hogan built in St. Paul was a decades-long attraction to crime. Hogan was in his mid 20s when he was first arrested in 1905, in his home state of California. By 1909, after several more jail stints in various states, he turned up in St. Paul. There, he realized he could take advantage of the sanctity offered by the O'Connor System, hiring crooks to carry out robberies and then fencing the goods from his new base. Hogan was also the key administrator of the system, as crooks new to town came to the Green Lantern to pay their respects—and a bribe—and learn their responsibility to keep their noses clean while in St. Paul.

As his crime empire grew, Hogan counted police officers and politicians as part of his circle, and a Bureau of Investigation report said Hogan's police informants let him know when one of his criminal associates was wanted elsewhere. Dapper Dan then had a chance to get the crooks into St. Paul, where they would be safe.

Through the 1920s, Hogan and his cohorts were responsible—or allegedly responsible—for robberies across the country. In 1922, Hogan disposed of some of the proceeds from a $200,000 robbery at the Denver Mint. Although no one was charged with the crime, the heist is credited to John Harvey Bailey, who came to St. Paul and gave Hogan $80,000 to launder. Hogan told Bailey, "It may take me a month or it may take me six months to dispose of this, but I'll get with it."[3] In his autobiography, the renowned bank robber Bailey expressed his satisfaction with Hogan's work.

The Green Lantern

John Harvey Bailey was a prolific bank robber who was said to have stolen more money from banks than John Dillinger. At different times, Bailey worked with Machine Gun Kelly and Alvin Karpis, two Depression-era crooks who also spent time in the Twin Cities. While in St. Paul, Bailey—like many others—hung out at the Green Lantern. According to crime historian Paul Maccabee, Bailey went by the name of Tom Brennan, and acted as the "resident professor of criminal techniques."[4] Along with serving as a classroom, the Green Lantern was a place where the underworld came to plan heists, dispose of their booty, and relax with a beer and some food. Under Dan Hogan's ownership, the menu featured hot dogs. Later on, the establishment's kitchen was known for its spaghetti and fried pork chops. During part of Prohibition, the beer came from an employee of the Schmidt Brewing Company, who funneled the alcohol from the brewery to his house through a secret tunnel. Most of the activity at the Green Lantern took place in a back-room speakeasy behind a fake wall, where visiting gangsters enjoyed music, gambling and exotic dancers along with their refreshments. Today, the former location of the Green Lantern at 545 North Wabasha is the site of public housing, complete with a library, where residents can read all about what once happened on the spot.

Hogan had a more direct role in other crimes, like a 1924 robbery of a collection wagon loaded with cash in St. Paul. Two years later, a report from the U.S. Post Office blamed Hogan for a series of Post Office robberies. And in 1927 he had been indicted for an earlier robbery that took place in South St. Paul. The charges were dropped when all the witnesses involved changed their story and refused to implicate Hogan. The Bureau of Investigation said the mass changes in heart could be traced to bribes or threats, courtesy of Hogan.

While undoubtedly a criminal mastermind, Hogan also earned some respect for the morality he seemingly brought to an immoral business. His word, some said, was as good as gold, and a newspaper article described his own way of enforcing order in St. Paul: "Police knew that he had frequently ordered thieves and gangsters out of the Twin Cities and sometimes gave them money so that they 'might be on their way.'"[5]

ODD DOINGS AT THE HOGAN HOUSE

Although Dan Hogan would say on his deathbed that he didn't have an enemy in the world, for a man who dealt with gangsters of all stripes, it paid to take precautions. That's why Hogan had an alarm system installed in his two-car garage at 1607 W. Seventh Street. But on the morning of December 4, 1928, the alarm's battery was dead, meaning anyone could slip into the garage undetected.

Early that morning, Hogan's wife Leila saw a strange car drive up to the house. Two men were inside; Mrs. Hogan didn't recognize them and paid them little attention. Police later speculated that these men were the ones who entered Hogan's garage, but no one knows for sure.

Someone, though, did enter the garage that morning, and they knew Hogan's habits. They planted a bomb under the hood of his coupe, not the larger sedan that sat next to it. The killers knew which one Hogan would take out that day. While the Hogans went about their business inside the house, the assassins did their work, placing a bomb under the car's floor near the rear of the engine. The bomb was wired to the car's starter, ready to blow as soon as Hogan turned the ignition.

Hogan drove a car similar to this one

It was approaching noon when Hogan made his way to the garage, after a large late breakfast. Joining him was his father-in-law, F. D. Hardy. Before they reached the car, the elder man realized he had left something in the house and he went back for it. Hogan entered the coupe alone, settled his somewhat corpulent body behind the wheel, and stepped on the starter pedal.

The blast was violent, shattering windows in the car and the garage. Its force bounced the coupe out of the garage and into the alley behind the house. The hood and steering wheel flew off and, as the *St. Paul Dispatch* reported, "holes in the steel sides of the car body showed where bits of metal had been buried through with the velocity of bullets."[6]

When his family and neighbors rushed to the scene, they found Hogan unconscious, his right hand mangled, his right leg almost completely ripped off his body, and blood everywhere. A relative later speculated that the blast might have taken off his head, if his large stomach hadn't forced him to lean back in the car seat to reach the pedals. An ambulance rushed Hogan to the hospital, where his leg was amputated. As news spread about the bombing and Hogan's need for a blood transfusion, potential donors streamed to the hospital. "Among them," the *Dispatch* said, "were racketeers, police characters and business men. These proffers of assistance were an indication of the esteem in which the murdered man was held by many people of the Twin Cities."[7]

Hogan regained consciousness for a time in the hospital and underwent the amputation without general anesthesia. For a time he seemed to regain some strength, but then he fell into a coma and died shortly before 9 p.m.

A GRAND FUNERAL AND GENERAL SPECULATION

The death of the St. Paul "godfather" spread across the country on the newspaper wires, with *The New York Times* headline referring to him as an "underworld ruler" who had another nickname: the "smiling peacemaker."[8] But in St. Paul, the killing sparked outrage over the city's general lawlessness, as the *Pioneer Press* rhetorically asked if the police ran the town, or the criminals. A wag might have answered in the affirmative for the latter.

Hogan's death spurred an outpouring of well-wishers, several thousand strong, to attend his wake, while others went to his funeral mass at St. Mary's Catholic Church in St. Paul. News reports said that mourners spent some $5,000 for flowers, with some coming from gangsters in New York and Chicago.

The question on many lips was, "Who had ordered the killing?" In early press articles, the police speculated that Hogan had been mixed up with gambling racketeers in Minnesota who wanted him gone. Perhaps they had hired New York gangsters to carry out the hit, or some New Yorkers might have even ordered the killing themselves, as payback for a murder of one of their own that Hogan had somehow been tied to.

As time went on, however, the focus turned to Harry "Dutch" Sawyer as the likely killer. Originally from Nebraska, Sawyer had, like Hogan, a string of arrests in other parts of the country before settling in St. Paul. There, he did some bootlegging and hooked up with Hogan, helping to sell some of the stolen goods that came through the Green Lantern. Sawyer's wife later claimed that he was swindled out of money by Hogan on several occasions. That, and the desire to take over as the St. Paul "don," supposedly fueled Sawyer's plot to have Hogan killed.

FBI

Harry Sawyer and his wife

There's no disputing that with Hogan gone, Sawyer became the purveyor of the Green Lantern and the man who kept the O'Connor System flourishing for several more years. Sawyer would also have close contact with some of the notorious gangsters who came to St. Paul during the early 1930s, serving as their "fixer" when they needed a new car or a gun. Sawyer, though, would never earn the respect, deserved or not, that Dapper Dan Hogan did.

A Favorite Madam

THE CRIME: Prominent men across the Twin Cities visit a famous brothel

PERPETRATOR: Nina Clifford, the madam of the house

SCENE OF THE CRIME: St. Paul

WHEN: From 1889 to 1929

Nina Clifford's home

Few figures in St. Paul's long history of crime are as legendary as Nina Clifford. Most historians who study her career as the most respected madam in Minnesota conclude that separating the myths from the reality is not easy. Even her real name is disputed: some say she was born Hannah Steinbrecher, while Paul Maccabee argues that this was Nina's married name before she began her life as a madam. He gives her maiden name as Crowe. But the sources seem to agree that she was born in Canada, came to Michigan as a child, then settled in St. Paul during the 1880s. And in St. Paul, she ran a bordello that catered to the city's elite, while at least one writer claimed she kept a second site that was reserved for "lumberjacks coming in from the woods to spend their hard-earned bucks."[1] Whatever their background, a wide range of men came to Nina's house, despite the crimes known to go on there. Or rather, because of them.

BUILDING A BUSINESS

In 1887, Nina Clifford bought two building lots on Washington Street in one of the oldest neighborhoods in St. Paul. Her neighbors in this area known as Uppertown included the county morgue and the police station. The permits for the buildings erected on the lots described them as "dwelling houses," though someone had added "and seminary" to one.[2] Clifford lived in the house at 145 Washington, while her workplace sat next door. The bordello was a fine, two-story brick building, costing some $12,000 to build, during an era when the average home cost much less. Inside, the house was well appointed, with plush carpeting and a marble fireplace—offering the kind of comfort Clifford's clients would come to expect. By the 1920s, business was so good that Clifford needed two phone lines to keep track of her affairs.

But the patrons at 147 Washington Street were not coming for the architecture or furnishings. They came to see Nina's girls, and by 1895 it seemed she had the most prosperous bordello in a neighborhood known for vices. Records from 1895 showed that Nina had 11 prostitutes, known as "sports" in the day, at the house, along with three servants. The 1900 Census showed two fewer working girls but more servants, including a musician. Business was good for Nina, who was known to accept diamonds as payment from high-rollers who lacked the cash to pay for her staff's services. Arthur Sundberg, who worked as a delivery boy during a part of the brothel's operating years, recalled being led to Clifford's desk, where she showed the teen a box filled with "several hundred unset diamonds . . . no small ones . . . She also had a dozen or more diamond rings with identification tags on each."[3]

Running a successful, albeit illegal, business did come with a price. Clifford and other area madams had to make regular appearances in municipal court to pay a fine. The fine was, in effect a licensing fee, since the police never made any effort to shut the operations down. Under police chief John "Big Fellow" O'Connor, Clifford and the others also paid direct bribes to the police. (Some historians speculate that O'Connor's wife may have run one of the Washington Street bordellos herself.)

Despite a legal system that mostly looked the other way at Clifford's endeavors, she did find herself arrested in 1913, as she was caught up in a corruption case involving deposed police chief Martin Flanagan and detective Fred Turner. Amid allegations of the police officers' graft, which included taking payments from "resort owners" and "women of the underworld" such as Clifford, the famous madam was indicted for bribery.[4] The next year, though, she was testifying for the prosecution and avoided conviction. Flanagan and Turner, however, both ended up in Stillwater State Prison.

LIFE ON WASHINGTON STREET

Along with female company, patrons at Clifford's house received food and beer. The beer probably came from the Bucket of Blood Saloon down the street (its name supposedly a reference to the frequent fights that broke out there). Some of the food came from the backyard, as chickens raised at the bordello ended up on the menu. Guests ate their meals off fine ceramic plates, while the girls used more common dinnerware. The girls, or perhaps the house's servants, sometimes threw their trash into the backyard.

Minnesota Historical Society

Nina Clifford's opulent Washington Street home

The women who worked for Clifford and the other St. Paul madams were usually young, and they made good money, compared to other women of the day. And Clifford generally treated them well, hiring taxis to take them to the beach at Lake McCarrons in Roseville. But half of the girls' earnings went to their madam, and the girls had to buy the fancy clothes and jewels they were expected to wear at work or when they went out on the town. And prostitution was unhealthy work, judging by the large number of medicine bottles unearthed during an archaeological dig at the site of Clifford's house in 1997. (Though rumor has it that for a time, the girls could receive check ups for sexually transmitted diseases at a discount at the nearby morgue.) Prostitutes, then as now, also faced violence from customers and fellow workers.

For Nina Clifford, though, her chosen profession proved safe and lucrative. She ran the house until her death, though by then business was declining. Still, she had amassed a fortune that she invested in Michigan, where she had family. She died of a stroke while visiting family there in 1929. Her ties to St. Paul's movers and shakers led to the rumor that a picture hanging in the former Minnesota Club on Washington Street is of Clifford, though that's not the case. An underground tunnel was also said to run from that once-storied private club to Clifford's house. Paul Maccabee, in his *John Dillinger Slept Here*, located a water tunnel that runs from the former club to within 100 feet of the bordello. The 1997 archaeological dig, however, saw no tunnel directly connected to Clifford's business.

While Clifford's patrons remain mostly unknown, her name was known, then and now. Her death made front-page news, and the excavation of her former property renewed interest in her and a time when St. Paul was known for lawlessness in many forms.

ABOUT THE STATE

News of Especial Interest to Minnesota Readers.

WOMEN TELL GRAFT STORIES

Astounding Disclosures of Alleged Corrupt Transactions in St. Paul's Underworld.

Clifford testifying about graft in St. Paul

ANOTHER NOTABLE MINNESOTA CRIME

BONNIE AND CLYDE VISIT OKABENA

Bonnie Parker and Clyde Barrow were among the most notorious bank robbers of the early 1930s. Like some of their fellow crooks, they spent time in Minnesota, though their crimes here were less spectacular. In 1932, Clyde and two gang members drove to Okabena to scout out a robbery of the bank there. Wintry roads convinced Clyde they should skip town, and instead they targeted a bank in Kansas. But the next year, the gang returned to Okabena during warmer weather and pulled off the heist. As the robbers made their getaway, some citizens opened fire on them, sparking a brief gun battle. No one was injured. Adding to Bonnie and Clyde's luck, three local residents were tried and wrongly convicted for carrying out the crime.

FBI

Bonnie and Clyde clown around

The Willmar Bank Robbery

Machine Gun Kelly

THE CRIME: A notorious gang robs the Bank of Willmar, shooting two

PERPETRATORS: Gang members include John Harvey Bailey, Verne Miller, and George "Machine Gun Kelly" Barnes

VICTIMS: Several bystanders

SCENE OF THE CRIME: Willmar

WHEN: July 15, 1930

FBI

The robbery of a small-town bank rarely seemed like "news" as the Great Depression began to pick up steam in 1930. What made the heist at the Bank of Willmar notable was that several of the most notorious gangsters of the era took part in it, and it shared some parallels with another Minnesota bank robbery of another era, the Northfield Raid of 1876. The aftermath of the Willmar robbery also showed the tendency for gangsters to turn on their own, leading to more mayhem in the region around St. Paul.

MACHINE GUN KELLY COMES TO MINNESOTA

Of the gangsters who took part in the Willmar robbery, the best known today to the general public is George Kelly Barnes, aka Machine Gun Kelly. A native of Tennessee, Barnes came from a wealthy family and spent time in college, studying agriculture, before turning to crime. He left school after falling in love and deciding to marry his first wife, Geneva Ramsey. The couple quickly had two kids, and as he struggled to pay the bills, Barnes turned to bootlegging for income.

After several arrests in Tennessee, Barnes began calling himself George Kelly and moved west with his family. The new name and locale didn't end his bad luck with the law; by 1930 Kelly had served time in the Leavenworth Federal Penitentiary, among other jail stops.

As with other crooks of the era, Kelly made friendships in Leavenworth that continued beyond the prison's walls. His new pals included Jimmy Keating and Tommy Holden, bank robbers who had worked together on the outside. One heist in 1926 netted them $130,000. Kelly was able to forge some documents that helped the pair walk out of Leavenworth unchallenged; Keating and Holden then headed for the safety of the O'Connor System in St. Paul. When Kelly was released from prison in 1930, he followed them there, and Keating and Holden invited Kelly to join their reconstituted gang for a robbery in Willmar, the seat of Kandiyohi County, about 100 miles west of the Twin Cities.

"Machine Gun" Gets His Name

By some accounts, Machine Gun Kelly got his moniker because he could spell out his name by firing bullets into a wall. But most agree he never used his trademark weapon to kill anyone. The aura that came to surround George Kelly and his Thompson submachine gun seems to have been in large part created by his second wife, Kathryn, whom he married in Minneapolis not long after the Willmar robbery. It was Mrs. Kelly, most historians say, who suggested her husband practice with a gun and who helped "market" the image of Machine Gun Kelly. Kathryn would take the spent cartridges from target practice and hand them out as souvenirs. Either the marketing or the practicing made an impression on the Bureau of Investigation: an August 1933 wanted poster for Kelly described him as an "expert machine gunner."[1] But expert or not, just Kelly's threats to mow down anyone who resisted him seemed to do the trick during his crimes.

A VIOLENT ROBBERY

The gang's target was the Bank of Willmar, which held some $3 million in deposits. Along with Kelly and the two gang leaders, the crew for the robbery included John Harvey Bailey and Sammy Silverman, a Kansas City thug. By some reports, Verne Miller was also there when the gang set out on July 15, 1930. Miller, from South Dakota, had once been a police officer and county sheriff in his home state. He started his criminal career in 1923 by embezzling government funds and fleeing to St. Paul; by 1933, the U.S. Justice Department was calling Miller "the most dangerous criminal in the country," connecting him to the murders of several people.[2] He would make other appearances in Minnesota, often with other famous criminals, before he was finally killed that year.

George Kelly's Tennessee mugshot

The gang pulled up to the Willmar bank shortly after 10:30 a.m., in a black Buick with plates that were stolen that morning. One member stayed behind in the car, while three went in with revolvers drawn. A fourth—perhaps Kelly—carried a machine gun and stood guard near the door. Sixteen employees were working there that morning, while nine customers carried out their banking business. Upon seeing the gunmen enter, several tellers pushed buttons that sounded alarms in the streets outside. As some people approached the bank, one of the gunmen kept them at bay.

Inside, one of the robbers yelled, "Lay down or we will kill you. We mean business." When a bank employee didn't move fast enough for the gang's liking, one of the robbers came over and began kicking him, demanding, "Hurry up and get down with the rest."[3] Despite the threats, two tellers snuck away and ran for the basement, where they took cover.

PEAU OF IDENTIFICATION
POLICE DEPARTMENT—DETECTIVE DIVISION
MEMPHIS, TENNESSEE

No. 15595

COLOR **WHITE**

DATE OF ARREST Sept. 26th 19:
DATE HANDLED Sept. 26th 19:

NAME **G E O R G E   K E L L Y   B A R N E S**
ALIAS George R. Kelly; R. G. Shannon; George Kelly; Thompson;
ALIAS George Barnes, etc.
ALIAS
CHARGE Fugitive(Kidnaper - Bootlegger - Stickup Man - Gangster (Wanted at Oklahoma City, Oklahoma in connection with the Urschel Kidnapping)

RESIDENCE At Large
HEIGHT 5'9 1/4" (B.Feet) AGE 37   WEIGHT 177   EYE Blue
COMPLEXION Fair   BUILD Medium Stout   OCCUPATION None
HAIR Blondine   MARRIED Yes   TEETH Good.
BORN Seattle, Washington July 17th 1896   OFFICER U.S.D.J. Agts. Rorer -   - Det.Sergts.
ARRESTED WITH Katherine Kelly, No. 15596; J. R. Tichenor, No. 15597 and S.E.Travis, No. 15598 a:
Langford P. Ramsey No. 15600.   Patrolman   and   MARKS, SCARS, MOLES, ETC.
I:- II:- III;- Dimple in chin.

All b7C

RTMENT—DETECTIVE DIVISION
MEMPHIS, TENNESSEE

COLOR **WHITE**

No. 1559

NAME **K A T H E R I N E   K E L L Y**
ALIAS Katherine Brooks - Katherine Thorn - Kathryn Kelly -
ALIAS
ALIAS

DATE OF ARREST Sept. 26th
DATE HANDLED Sept. 26th

CHARGE Fugitive(Wife of George R. Kelly No. 15595.)
RESIDENCE At Large

HEIGHT 5'6 3/8" (B.F.) AGE 29
COMPLEXION Fair   BUILD Slender   WEIGHT 130   EYE Dark Slate Gray
HAIR Auburn   MARRIED Yes   OCCUPATION None
BORN Tupelo, Mississippi March 18th 1904   OFFICER U.S.D.J. Agts. Rorer -   TEETH Good.
ARRESTED WITH George R. Kelly, No. 15595; J. C. Tichenor, No. 15597   - Patrolman   and   - Det. Sergts.   S. A. Travis, No. 15598
Langford P. Ramsey No. 15600.   MARKS, SCARS, MOLES, ETC.
I:- II:- III:- Faint out scar on Right Cheekbone, Faint vert. cut scar at inner end Right
brow. Dimple in chin.

All b7C

FBI

Rapsheets for George Kelly and his wife, Katherine

Several of the crooks then made for the tellers' drawers, grabbing cash and securities. While the scene unfolded inside, dozens of Willmar residents began gathering outside, responding to the alarms ringing through downtown. The machine-gun toting robbers threatened to kill anyone who got too close to the building.

The whole operation, witnesses guessed, took about eight minutes. One teller was impressed, telling a reporter, "The bandits certainly were thorough in their work. They were not amateurs."[4] One teller must have interfered with that work, as he received a pistol-whipping for his trouble. Then, heading outside and into their waiting car, the gang ran into troubles of its own.

Two local residents, gas station attendant Sam Evans and jeweler H. S. Paffrath, had arrived on the scene with pistols. As the robbers jumped into the car, the two men began to fire. One bullet struck the getaway driver, who slumped over at the wheel. Another robber then slid his way into the driver's seat. A second robber was wounded as well, and the gunfire from both sides left the Buick's rear window shattered and broken glass from storefronts on the street. The shooting also wounded two bystanders, one seriously, though she recovered from her wounds.

ON THE LAM

With their car "shot up pretty bad," as Bailey later put it, the gang headed west out of Willmar.[5] One report put them in Henderson, where they supposedly bandaged up their wounded. Then the robbers went to Minneapolis, where they ditched their car and transferred the loot—about $142,000—into another car and headed to St. Paul.

The Willmar crime sparked outrage in the local press. Both the *Pioneer Press* and W. F. Rhinow, head of the state's Bureau of Criminal Apprehension, compared it to the work of the Jesse James gang decades before. Rhinow said the modern-day gangsters and the James-Younger boys shared a "daring and cold-blooded disregard for human life."[6]

There were similarities between the Willmar robbery and the Northfield raid. In both cases, a teller was wounded; citizens bravely stepped forward to engage the crooks in a gun battle; and several of the robbers were wounded in the shootout. But unlike the Northfield robbery, the criminals did not take time beforehand to case out the targeted bank and town. And unlike the Northfield raid, none of the robbers in 1930 faced justice for their crime.

ONE DEAD ROBBER

Sammy Silverman, though, did not have long after the July robbery to take part in any others. On the night of August 13, acting on a tip that gangsters were hanging out near White Bear Lake, BCA head Rhinow found the dead bodies of two Kansas City crooks. A search the next morning turned up Silverman's body too. All three had been shot at close range, Silverman behind the right ear. Press reports noted that Silverman had been a suspect in the Willmar robbery, as well as in the killing of a Kansas City police officer. The police thought the slayings were connected to a gangland squabble over money from slot machines, and Chicago's George "Bugs" Moran was mentioned as a suspect. The truth of the killings, as much as it's known, ties the murders to another of the Willmar robbers.

Several years later, Machine Gun Kelly claimed that Verne Miller was the trigger-man. Silverman had somehow crossed Miller after the Willmar robbery, and Miller killed him in retribution. The other two slain men, Kansas City gangsters, just happened to be with Silverman when the confrontation occurred. Miller was never arrested for that murder or the others he carried out; his career after Willmar led him afoul of the Mob in several cities, and some underworld figure ordered his death.

As for Kelly, he explained the Silverman killing while in prison, after his conviction for the crime that ended his career, the 1933 kidnapping of Oklahoma oilman Charles Urschel. Kelly spent time in Alcatraz before dying in Leavenworth in 1954.

The "G-men"

If Machine Gun Kelly's prowess with a Tommy gun was something of a myth, crediting him with coining a well-known phrase was even more of one. For decades, the story went that Kelly was the first person to call J. Edgar Hoover's agents "G-men," or "Government men." Actually, G-men was already a slang term for government agents in any department, not just the Bureau of Investigation. The myth that developed said that as he faced capture after the Urschel kidnapping, Kelly said, "Don't shoot, G-men, don't shoot!"[7]

According to Bureau of Investigation records, Kelly didn't say anything when he was apprehended in Memphis, Tennessee, but he did have his hands in the air. Several months later, a newspaper reported that Kelly feared the "G's" would have slaughtered him if he had resisted arrest. Even later, another journalist passed along the supposed Kelly quote of "Don't shoot, G-men." The legend lives on, though the FBI debunks it on its website.

ANOTHER NOTABLE MINNESOTA CRIME

A FAMOUS KIDNAPPING WITH LOCAL TIES

When Charles A. Lindbergh, Jr. made his historic 1927 transatlantic flight, Minnesotans felt pride for someone they saw as a native son, since the aviator had spent his boyhood in Little Falls when his father represented the area's district in the U.S. House of Representatives. Then, when news of the kidnapping of Lindbergh's baby son spread across the country in 1932, Minnesotans

The Lindbergh ransom note

The missing poster for the Lindbergh baby

closely followed the story. The day after the kidnapping, Governor Floyd Olson said that "the people of your home state are shocked to learn of the cruel removal of your infant child from your home."[1] The shock was even greater in the town of Little Falls. And for a time later in the year, a gangster who ended up in St. Paul was considered a possible suspect in the kidnapping. But that crook, Abe Wagner, had his own troubles that year. (See page 80.)

Snatching Millionaires

FBI

Alvin "Creepy" Karpis

THE CRIME: Twin Cities beer magnates William Hamm Jr. and Edward Bremer are kidnapped and held for ransom, which is paid

PERPETRATORS: The Barker-Karpis Gang

VICTIM: William Hamm Jr.; Edward Bremer

SCENE OF THE CRIME: Hamm is abducted near Minnehaha Avenue and Greenbrier Street in St. Paul; Bremer is taken at South Lexington Parkway and Goodrich Avenue, St. Paul

WHEN: June 15, 1933, for Hamm; January 17, 1934, for Bremer

Of all the gangsters who holed up in St. Paul during its heyday as a crooks' paradise, Alvin Karpis may have done the most to burnish the city's dubious reputation. In his 1971 autobiography, he wrote, "Every criminal of any importance in the 1930s made his home at one time or another in St. Paul. If you were looking for a guy you hadn't seen for a few months, you usually thought of two places—prison or St. Paul."[1]

Karpis, of course, was more than just an ex-con with a memoirist's flair. He earned the nickname Creepy, supposedly for his evil-eye glare. And for a time before his arrest in 1936, Karpis was Public Enemy Number One, in part for his role in pulling off two sensational kidnappings in St. Paul a few years earlier. (Various robberies and murders in several states fleshed out his criminal credentials.) Working with the Barker brothers—Arthur ("Doc") and Fred—and several other crooks, Karpis and his gang engineered their own crime wave that lasted for five years. From simple burglary, Karpis and his accomplices worked their way up to bank robberies, before deciding to turn to kidnapping.

GRABBING MR. HAMM

Karpis first met Fred Barker in 1930, when both were serving time in the Kansas State Penitentiary. After getting out of prison the next year, they committed their first crime together. For a time at the end of 1931, Karpis lived with Barker, his mother Kate and her boyfriend, in Missouri. When the two young men's crimes—including their killing of a sheriff—began to catch up with them in the area, they took the advice of a family friend and headed for St. Paul.

After a stint in Kansas City, Karpis, Baker and their growing gang took refuge in White Bear Lake, which served as a base of operations for a robbery in Kansas. Soon after, Doc Barker joined the criminal enterprise. At the end of 1932, notorious killer Verne Miller was also part of the gang, which had a bloody shootout as it robbed a Minneapolis bank. Two police officers and a bystander were killed by the crooks' machine guns.

The "Brains" Behind the Gang?

For decades, many popular accounts of the Barker-Karpis gang stressed the role of Ma Barker in planning, if not taking part, in its crimes. The reality was not so dramatic for the mother of two of the most notorious gangsters of the 1930s. Arizona Barker, known as Kate, certainly knew about her sons' criminal doings, but she was, in the words of Alvin Karpis, "generally law abiding."[2] John Harvey Bailey said she was usually in another room when jobs were planned, and that she couldn't organize breakfast, let alone a crime wave. But after her death (at the hands of the FBI), J. Edgar Hoover played up her role as the brains behind the Barker-Karpis gang—a claim not backed up by internal FBI documents. Today, even the FBI publicly admits that Barker was no criminal mastermind, though it blames her inflated legend on the media, not its own former director.

Fred Barker, Doc Barker, and Alvin Karpis

Through the end of 1932 and the start of the New Year, the gang members hopscotched across the country, spending time in Reno, Chicago and the Twin Cities. By late spring, Fred Barker was in St. Paul with a new girlfriend, while Karpis and the others rented a cottage at Bald Eagle Lake. At the suggestion of Jack Peifer, an associate of St. Paul criminal fixer Harry Sawyer, the gang was going to attempt its first kidnapping. Helping out would be Fred Goetz, a Chicago mobster who worked for Al Capone. The target: William Hamm Jr.

During the 1860s, German immigrant Theodore Hamm had taken over a small brewery in St. Paul's Swede Hollow and turned it into a major company. William Jr., his grandson, was president of the family brewing business in 1933, and Karpis and the gang began carefully preparing for their "snatch." He and Fred Barker ventured almost daily into the city to study Hamm's routine and case the brewery and his home. Karpis later wrote, "We got to know so much about the guy that I was sick of him long before the kidnapping."[3]

By June 15, the details of the plan were in place. Karpis would pose as a chauffeur behind the wheel of the abduction car, while an elder bank robber, Charlie Fitzgerald, would approach Hamm on the street as he made his daily noontime walk between his mansion and the brewery. The ransom was set at $100,000, an easy sum for a brewing family to produce now that Prohibition was finally over.

The operation rolled smoothly along, with Fitzgerald greeting Hamm in a friendly manner, then calmly directing him to the waiting car. Once inside it, Hamm found himself wearing goggles filled with cotton so he couldn't see where his kidnappers were taking him. After a stop in Wisconsin, where the gang forced Hamm to write several ransom notes, they took him to their ultimate destination, a safe house in Bensenville, Illinois.

At the house, Karpis let Hamm read magazines and offered him beer. There was no Hamm's in the fridge, and Karpis, not wanting to offend his victim, soaked the labels off the bottles of the competing brand, only to learn that the brewery president couldn't tell his product from anyone else's. Overall the kidnappers treated Hamm well, and they didn't try to hide their identities. They merely told the brewer to look at the wall when they brought him food. Hamm, though, was able to sneak a few peeks of his captors.

FREEDOM

The man Hamm chose to carry out the ransom negotiations on his behalf was an employee named William Dunn. As Paul Maccabee explains in his *John Dillinger Slept Here*, Dunn was more than just a brewery worker; a former local business owner, he had longstanding ties to the Twin Cities underworld, and sometimes delivered payments from the crooks to the St. Paul police force. Under oath, Dunn would later admit he had been friends with Peifer, the man who orchestrated the Hamm kidnapping. The dealings that men like Dunn had with the local criminals, Maccabee writes, "reveal how permeable the walls were in St. Paul between 'civilized' society and the gangsters."[4]

Dunn received a call from the kidnappers with a demand for the ransom. They wanted it in small bills, telling Dunn, "Be sure you see that the money is not marked."[5] Dunn started to protest that he couldn't get that kind of money, but the line went dead. He then received notes detailing how he should leave the money. Helping the kidnappers was a bought St. Paul cop—none other than the chief of police, Tom Brown. The chief passed along tips about the doings of the Bureau of Investigation, helping the kidnappers avoid falling into any traps. In another note, the gang made itself clear: "Get away from the coppers . . . if you try to out s[m]art us you will only prolong the agony."[6]

Finally, on June 19, the deal was made in Wyoming, Minnesota: Karpis and his gang got their money, and Hamm was released. The gang then continued

A vintage Hamm's ad

its wandering ways from the year before, heading first to Illinois and then back to Reno, though they took time to come back to Minnesota to pull off a $30,000 heist in South St. Paul that left one police officer dead. Meanwhile, the police arrested members of a Chicago gang led by Roger "Terrible" Touhy for the Hamm kidnapping. Touhy and his crew were acquitted later that year, with Hamm's failure to identify them as his kidnappers playing a part.

The Prints Don't Lie

While Terrible Touhy was awaiting his trial, the Bureau of Investigation continued to study evidence from the Hamm kidnapping. In September 1933, its Crime Lab successfully demonstrated a new technique for the first time. In what is now called latent fingerprint identification, the technicians used silver nitrate to pick up fingerprints on surfaces that wouldn't reveal prints when dusted with simple powder. The Crime Lab found prints on the Hamm ransom notes—prints belonging to Alvin Karpis and other members of the gang. This confirmed their participation in the kidnapping, though the Touhy trial went on.

THE BREMER KIDNAPPING

By the end of 1933, Karpis, the Barkers, and others in the gang were back in Minnesota and planning another kidnapping. This time the target was Edward Bremer, a banker who also had family ties to another local brewery, Schmidt. His father, one of the richest men in the Twin Cities, was also a personal friend of President Franklin D. Roosevelt, a fact that didn't deter Fred Barker. The gang had been facing heat from law enforcement since 1931; how much worse could it get?

The crime took place on January 17, 1934. Once again, the gang knew its victim's routine: Each morning, Bremer drove his daughter Hertzy to her private school on South Lexington Parkway. On the 17th, after he dropped her off, Bremer halted at a stop sign, only to see a man approach his car with a gun.

Another man entered from the other side of the car and struck Bremer in the head. The men sped off in the car and took Bremer to Illinois. They soon sent a ransom note to Bremer's friend Walter Magee. This time the gang upped the ante, demanding $200,000. And Karpis and the rest warned against any police involvement: "You better take care of the payoff first and let them do the detecting later."[7] Bremer added his signature at the end of the note, telling Magee that he was responsible for the banker's safety, and the Bremers would take care of the money.

Bremer's father Adolph asked the police to heed the request to stand down until Edward was released. But law enforcement officials at every level investigated, with J. Edgar Hoover particularly interested in the second sensational kidnapping to hit the Twin Cities. The feds wiretapped Bremer's house and the Schmidt brewery.

Over the course of several days, the gang sent more ransom notes. At times during his captivity Bremer was blindfolded, so he couldn't get a good look at his captors. But Bremer listened carefully to the ambient sounds around him and studied details in his room. His observations would later help the Bureau of Investigation identify his kidnappers.

FREEDOM AND PRISON

Negotiations for Bremer's release went on into February. Finally, on the 6th, Walter Magee picked up a car the kidnappers left for him and filled it with the ransom money Adolph Bremer had agreed to pay. Along with the money, the elder Bremer included a note that said in part, "Now, boys, I am counting on your honor. Be sports and do the square thing and turn Ed loose immediately . . ."[8] Following the kidnapper's instructions, Magee headed to Farmington and followed a bus heading to Rochester. He was just outside Zumbrota when he saw a prearranged signal that meant he should stop the car and drop off the money. The next day, a sore and dazed Bremer was released in Rochester and made his way back to his hometown.

With Bremer's release, law officials promised a massive manhunt to track down the kidnappers. One clue that Bremer provided helped the Bureau of Investigation track down gas cans that had been used to fuel one of the gang's cars. A print lifted from one of the cans belonged to Doc Barker. Other clues confirmed Karpis's role in the crime, so the Bureau knew whom to look for; now it was just a question of finding them.

FBI

Alvin Karpis shows his surgically removed fingerprints

With the heat on them once again, the gang shuttled some of the ransom money from one hiding place to another, and Karpis and Fred Barker sought a doctor's help in altering their faces and fingerprints. The latter operation succeeded, but the facial surgery failed, and the procedures left Barker howling in pain like a "raving maniac."[9] For a time, Karpis and his girlfriend lived in Cleveland, then journeyed to Cuba, where Fred and his mother later joined them. By early 1935, they were in Florida, while Doc Barker was in Chicago. There, on January 8, the Feds arrested Doc. Meanwhile, acting on tip from an informant, the Bureau prepared to arrest the gang members hiding out in Florida.

On January 16, 1935, the FBI closed in on a cottage rented by Ma and Fred Barker. A shootout ensued, leaving both gang members dead. Karpis heard of the shootings and headed north, to Atlantic City. He managed to shoot his way out of an attempted arrest, wounding several officers in the process. Already named Public Enemy Number One, Karpis began a new crime spree as he traveled across the country, trying to elude arrest. Finally, on May 1, 1936, FBI special agents apprehended him in New Orleans, with J. Edgar Hoover himself on the scene (though by Karpis's account, Hoover hid behind a building while his men made the arrest). Karpis then made one last trip to St. Paul, to face charges for the Hamm kidnapping. His conviction for that crime led to a stretch at Alcatraz. When he was finally released, Karpis headed to Spain, where he died in 1979.

One Who Got Away

THE CRIME: St. Paul police and Bureau of
Investigation agents confront John Dillinger

PERPETRATORS: John Dillinger, his girlfriend
Evelyn "Billie" Frechette, and gang member
Homer Van Meter

SCENE OF THE CRIME: Lincoln Court Apartments,
St. Paul

FBI

John Dillinger

WHEN: March 31, 1934

For a brief time during 1933 and 1934, John Dillinger caught the national eye like few criminals before him. His claim to fame as the federal government's "Public Enemy Number One" came after his last stay in Minnesota. But Dillinger's exploits in the state helped him earn that distinction, along with a string of robberies, shootings and jailbreaks across the Midwest.

Yet with all his lawlessness, Dillinger was careful to obey the code of St. Paul's "O'Connor System," an arrangement set up during the early 1900s between then-St. Paul police chief John O'Connor and gangsters, hoodlums and crooks of all stripes (see page 46). Dillinger's adherence to the code meant that he could come to St. Paul for medical treatment or just to lie low between crimes, which he did several times during March 1934.

Fresh from a jailbreak in Crown Point, Indiana, Dillinger set off on a new crime wave that featured robberies in South Dakota and Iowa, car thefts, and the wounding of a motorcycle cop. During the month, Dillinger and his girlfriend Evelyn "Billie" Frechette spent some time in Minneapolis, and he and his gang also hung out at the Green Lantern, St. Paul's notorious crooks' watering hole on Wabasha Street. Some reports from the era also placed Dillinger at other spots in Minnesota, such as Big Marine Lake in Washington

County, where he bought milk from a local farmer, and Scandia, where he and several gang members visited a tavern.

But the most meaningful Minnesota location for Dillinger would be 93 South Lexington Parkway in St. Paul, site of the Lincoln Court Apartments. There, only luck and some sloppy police work kept Dillinger from being caught several months before he earned the designation of Public Enemy Number One.

THE PATH TO ST. PAUL

Dillinger's career of crime had begun ten years earlier in his home state of Indiana. Barely 21 and newly married, Dillinger and an accomplice robbed a grocery store but were quickly arrested. Taking his father's advice and pleading guilty, Dillinger was stunned by the stiff sentence he received: up to 20 years in prison. Later, after one of the bank robberies that sparked his rise as a true gangster, Dillinger wrote his father that his harsh and unexpected punishment shaped his future life of crime: "I guess I did too much time, for where I went in a carefree boy, I came out bitter toward everything in general . . . if I had gotten off more leniently when I made my first mistake this would never have happened."[1]

During his first stint in prison, Dillinger made clothes, played baseball, and met some of his later criminal cohorts, including Homer van Meter. In 1933, he was paroled, and almost immediately robbed a bank in Ohio and was arrested. While he was in jail, some of Dillinger's prison buddies broke out of the Indiana penitentiary (using guns that Dillinger had provided while he was free), then sprung him from his new cell. Together, they started a crime wave that included robbing banks and storming police stations to steal weapons and bulletproof vests.

A Highly Perfected Craft

Craftsmen of all trades have long passed on their skills to the next generation, and bank robbers of the twentieth century were no exception. John Dillinger could trace his robbery lineage to Herman Lamm, a former German military officer who immigrated to the United States and supposedly hooked up for a time with remnants of Butch Cassidy and the Sundance Kid's Wild Bunch. Known as "the Baron," Lamm established the modern formula for carefully casing banks and planning detailed escape routes before a heist. Dillinger learned the "Lamm method" in prison from Walter Dietrich, who had worked with Lamm. The Baron successfully used his method for several years before being killed in a shootout in 1930.

The Dillinger gang's luck ran out on January 24, 1934, in Tucson, Arizona. They seemed to have headed there to let the heat from police cool down in the Midwest. But during their stay, they were recognized from wanted posters and arrested, with Dillinger amazed he was nabbed by "hick town" cops.[2] He was soon back in jail in Indiana, facing a murder charge for killing a police officer during an earlier robbery. But once again, Dillinger didn't stay behind bars for long. He claimed he whittled a piece of wood into the shape of a gun and used it to force his guards to release him. Bribes arranged by his lawyer might have also helped open the doors of his cell. With another escapee, Dillinger grabbed several machine guns and took off in a hijacked car.

As Dillinger made his way to Chicago, the Minnesota newspapers joined others around the country in announcing Dillinger's escape. *The Albert Lea Evening Journal's* March 3 front page blared, "Dillinger Escapes from Indiana County Jail," calling it a "daring dash."[3] Readers there and across the state didn't know the role Minnesota would soon play in the gangster's saga.

LIFE IN THE TWIN CITIES

After a brief stay in Chicago, where he had time to visit with Billie Frechette, Dillinger headed for the Twin Cities. Gang member Homer Van Meter had rented an apartment in Minneapolis, and he was part of a new gang that Dillinger now joined. Also in the group was a machine-gun-toting thug named

Lester Gillis—better known today as Baby Face Nelson. Nelson might have seen himself as the head of this new gang, but when it began robbing banks, the press quickly dubbed it Dillinger's.

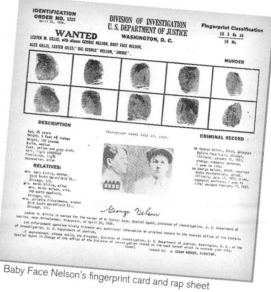

Baby Face Nelson's fingerprint card and rap sheet

Using Minneapolis as its initial base, the reconstituted Dillinger crew struck first in Sioux Falls, South Dakota. With the rest of the gang outside, Dillinger, Van Meter and Nelson entered the bank, guns drawn. As an alarm bell rang, they grabbed the cash they could then bolted for the getaway car—but not before Nelson wounded a motorcycle cop who had arrived on the scene. The gang made off with $46,000 then headed back to Minnesota.

By this time, Dillinger had a new worry. With the earlier theft of a car in Indiana, and then driving it across state lines to Illinois, he had broken a federal law. In Washington, J. Edgar Hoover of the Bureau of Investigation (soon to be renamed the FBI) now had legal grounds to set his men on Dillinger's trail. In charge of the manhunt was Melvin Purvis, a highly regarded agent based in Chicago. The Bureau's first wanted poster for Dillinger appeared on March 12.

The next day, Dillinger and his gang headed to Mason City, Iowa, for their next robbery. They managed to take a slightly larger haul, but paid for it in blood. A shootout in the street outside the bank left Dillinger and another gang member wounded. After a brief detour to Chicago, Dillinger and three of his gang drove to St. Paul, where they ended up on the doorstep of Dr. Nels Mortensen. On the surface, the doctor seemed like a model citizen: He commanded an American Legion post and served as the head of the Minnesota

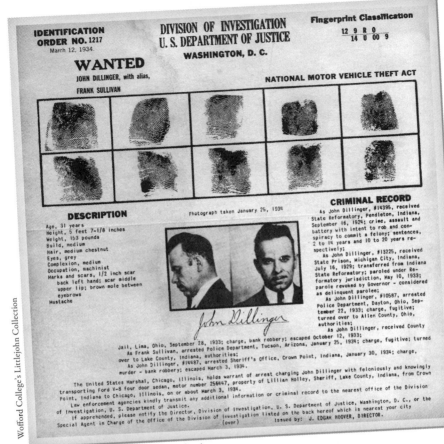

Dillinger's fingerprint card and rap sheet

State Board of Health. But Mortensen had become caught up in the corruption and criminal activity that flourished in the city. During a local political race, he took campaign money from a known underworld associate, and in several instances he helped criminals. Mortensen, though, later adamantly insisted to the Bureau of Investigation that he didn't know that the man who came to his door on the 14th with a wounded shoulder was John Dillinger.

Mortensen patched up Dillinger and the wound responded well. Within a few days, Frechette was in St. Paul, where she rented apartment 303 at Lincoln Court for herself and Dillinger. Rent was $60 per month, and the couple went by the names of Mr. and Mrs. Carl Hellman.

SHOWDOWN ON LEXINGTON PARKWAY

For almost two weeks, the "Hellmans" tried to live a quiet life. They visited a local bakery and went to the movies at the Uptown, a now-demolished theater. Dillinger was known as a movie buff and saw films at various Twin Cities theaters during his visits there. (Frechette said he was partial to the Disney cartoon *The Three Little Pigs*.) Frechette acted as a housewife for the gang, cooking for them and doing other domestic chores. Hanging clothes outside to dry, she caught the attention of neighborhood boys, as she ventured out wearing red shorts and a halter top. Decades later, one of those boys said, "We'd never seen women in shorts and halters before. So we'd whistle at Dillinger's girl from the distance."[4]

Trying to create an image of normalcy was no easy task for a wanted criminal and his gang. Daisy Coffey, landlady at the Lincoln Court Apartments, noticed suspicious behavior from the occupants of #303. She went to the local Bureau of Investigation office, reporting how the Hellmans rarely left the building, and when they did, they went through the back door. They also seemed to have frequent guests, and someone else may have been living with them. Coffey also reported the Hellmans' tendency to keep the shades drawn for long stretches, and their refusal to allow a maintenance person into the apartment.

Coffey's information led the local agents to stake out Dillinger's apartment. Then, on March 31, two federal agents and St. Paul detective Henry Cummings paid a visit to the Hellmans. Cummings and G-man Rufus Coulter went inside the building while Agent Rosser Nalls stayed out front. No one watched the back door.

At 10.15 a.m., Agent Coulter knocked on the door to apartment 303. Frechette opened the door just a crack and the two men said they wanted to see her husband Carl. Frechette said he was out but would be back later in the day. The law officials then asked to speak with her; she stalled for time. With the door closed again, Dillinger told her to grab a bag and get ready to run, while he prepared a machine gun to aid in their escape.

While this was going on, Homer Van Meter entered the apartment building through the rear door. Reaching Dillinger's apartment, he saw the two men outside it. They questioned him: who was he, what was he doing. Van Meter concocted a story that gave him the chance to go back outside. Coulter, though, soon trailed after him, and found Van Meter in the basement stairs, gun in hand. Van Meter fired, missed and ran, with Coulter now after him with his gun drawn. With both men running and firing, Van Meter somehow managed to escape without being hit.

Back in #303, Dillinger heard the shooting and opened the door slightly, sticking the muzzle of his machine gun outside. As a Bureau of Investigation report said, Dillinger "began spraying the hallway with bullets."[5] Cummings hid in an alcove and fired his gun but he couldn't keep Dillinger and Frechette from escaping down the unguarded back stairway. Outside the building, Frechette bolted to the nearby garage where the couple kept their black Hudson. Gun in one hand, suitcase in another, and blood flowing from a gunshot in his calf, Dillinger jumped into the car.

LAST DAYS IN MINNESOTA

The two sped off to the Minneapolis apartment of fellow gang member Eddie Green. Frechette later wrote that Dillinger "sat there in the back seat of the car frowning and holding his leg."[6] At the apartment, Frechette went with Green's wife Beth while the two men sought a doctor. They enlisted the services of Clayton May, who, like Mortensen, had associated with crooks before. May, though, later claimed that only Dillinger's

Two FBI handouts for John Dillinger

threat to "blow your head off" led him to help the fugitive.[7] May, Green and Dillinger went to the home of May's nurse, Augusta Salt. May treated the wound and told Dillinger to rest. He and Frechette stayed at Salt's until April 4.

Meanwhile, in the streets of the Twin Cities, police and federal agents searched for the fugitive. Others waited to see if he would return to his old Chicago stomping grounds. Instead, the couple headed for Dillinger's family homestead in Mooresville, Indiana. Frechette didn't think that was a good idea, but Dillinger insisted, saying, "Listen Billie, who's smarter—me or the cops?"[8]

After the escape to Mooresville, Dillinger and Frechette briefly returned to Chicago, where the Bureau of Investigation nabbed the moll while Dillinger escaped. He and Van Meter committed one robbery in Indiana, then Dillinger and his gang had a shootout in Wisconsin with the Bureau of Investigation. Returning to Minnesota, Dillinger, Van Meter and a third gang member engaged in a rolling shootout with local police, with Dillinger blasting away at the trailing cops through his car's knocked-out rear window. Managing to escape once again, he then headed back to Chicago.

While the manhunt went on, newspapers detailed the exploits of Dillinger. In the era of the Great Depression, some people championed Dillinger's assault on banks, though he was hardly the "Robin Hood" figure a few tried to make him out to be. The trail of dead bodies he and his gang left behind was proof of that. But there was no question that his anti-hero image appealed to some, even as J. Edgar Hoover used the Dillinger case to boost the respect and fame of his Bureau of Investigation.

In May, while the Bureau of Investigation kept up its search for Dillinger, Frechette stood trial in St. Paul for harboring a fugitive. She was convicted and received a two-year prison sentence, as did Dr. May for his role in aiding the gangster. Eddie Green's wife, Beth, received a slightly shorter sentence, though Eddie had already been gunned down by Bureau of Investigation agents. By one account, Dillinger showed up in St. Paul to see how the trial was going before going back on the lam. At the least, he was paying for Frechette's legal fees. But soon Dillinger had another girlfriend, and he and the gang had more crimes to commit. Dillinger's life of murder and mayhem

The Biograph Theater, where Dillinger was gunned down

finally came to an end outside Chicago's Biograph Theater. Working on an informant's tip, Melvin Purvis and his men found Dillinger there on July 22. Dillinger spotted the agents and fled, but this time he could not escape their bullets. He died on the street, Public Enemy Number One no more.

ANOTHER NOTABLE MINNESOTA CRIME

MURDER, INC., COMES TO ST. PAUL

Abe Wagner ran a small bootlegging operation in New York. When he crossed a powerful gang there in 1932, one with ties to crime boss Lucky Luciano, he fled for his life and turned up in St. Paul. But he couldn't escape the grasp of Murder, Inc., a squad of hitmen financed by Meyer Lansky and Bugsy Siegel, among others. Murder, Inc., could be trusted to kill rival criminals anywhere in the country, as they proved with Wagner. Although living under a new name and working as a fruit seller, Wagner could not evade the two men Murder, Inc., sent for him. The killers found him walking on University Avenue, shot him on the sidewalk, then followed him into the Green Dragon, where they finished the hit. The murderers were caught, and despite the financial pull of the crime syndicate behind Murder, Inc., they were convicted and received life sentences.

Meyer Lansky

Beating the Rap—As Usual

Kid Cann

THE CRIME: Lifelong criminal figure is charged with murdering journalist Walter W. Liggett

PERPETRATOR: Isadore Blumenfeld, aka Kid Cann

VICTIM: Walter W. Liggett

SCENE OF THE CRIME: Minneapolis

WHEN: Murder occurred on December 9, 1935

Many major, colorful underworld figures passed through the Twin Cities during the heyday of the gangster era, but none spent his formative years there and then made the region his home for most of his life—except Kid Cann. Born Isadore Blumenfeld to the son of Romanian immigrants, he came to Minneapolis when he was only two. Like many immigrant kids in big cities, he was exposed to a rough lifestyle on the streets, but he made his way up the ladder, becoming a rising star of the underworld. He built an empire based on bootlegging, leading a group of criminals known as the Combination. Later he extended his reach into the sales of legal liquor, prostitution and gambling, and by 1942, the FBI said he was the "overlord of the Minneapolis, Minnesota, underworld."[1]

By that time, Cann had been indicted several times but always managed to escape punishment, usually by throwing around bribes or making threats. The fortune he amassed through his illegal activities helped Cann win friends in high places, including in the halls of government. And those ties to political leaders may have led to Cann's role in the death of journalist Walter Liggett—despite what a Minneapolis jury found in 1936.

MAKING ENEMIES

To some, Walter Liggett was a crusader fighting against corruption in Minnesota during a particularly corrupt era. To others, he was the publisher of a "scandal sheet" that besmirched those in power. Despite the latter criticism, Liggett was a talented journalist who saw his byline appear in respected periodicals. He was also a dedicated progressive who wanted to thwart government's abuse of power and its ties to criminal elements. A Minnesota native, Liggett helped form the state's Farmer-Labor Party before heading off to New York to begin his writing career. He returned to his home state with his family in 1933, bent on using his muckraking skills to improve life there. With help from Governor Floyd Olson, Liggett bought a small weekly based in Red Wing and renamed it the *Midwest American*. The paper was meant to support Farmer-Labor goals and Olson's policies, and Liggett later moved its base to Rochester.

Governor Floyd Olson

By 1934, Liggett found himself increasingly at odds with his patron, the governor. Olson reacted with a heavy hand to strikes in Minneapolis, including issuing a gag order on local newspapers. The attempt to stifle freedom of the press led the *Chicago Tribune* to compare him to the Nazis. Although Liggett disliked Olson's imposition of martial law, he especially took the governor to task for increasingly cozying up to the state's corporate and underworld interests. And Liggett believed another journalist who spoke out against Olson, Howard Guilford, was "shot down in cold blood by hired gunmen because he dared expose some ramifications of Floyd Olson with the underworld."[2] The powers-that-be tried to paint Guilford as a blackmailer who was killed for his misdeeds, not his journalism.

ANOTHER JOURNALIST KILLED

Olson won reelection in 1934, and the next year Liggett increasingly called for his impeachment. Despite the growing animosity between him and the governor, Liggett thought that he would escape Guilford's fate. But he was wrong. On December 9, as his young daughter and wife watched from the family car, Walter Liggett was shot five times with a machine gun. As neighbors began to crowd the alley and his crying wife kneeled beside him, Liggett died. The killers sped away, but not before Mrs. Liggett got a look at the two men inside. And one of them, she insisted, was Kid Cann.

The next day the national press reported the killing and the arrest of Cann and Meyer Schuldberg, a Cann associate in the now-legal liquor business. *The New York Times* said that Schuldberg had recently threatened Liggett to stop writing about Cann and organized crime's ties to politicians. The journalist had also just accused Cann of being one of several men who had severely beaten him during the fall. Based on the testimony of Mrs. Liggett and another eyewitness, Cann was soon indicted for the murder, but within several weeks the *Times* noted a lack of any real effort in Minneapolis to address some of the corruption Liggett had reported. "There apparently is going to be no housecleaning . . . it is even reported that in a quiet way the gambling places are reopening and the slot machines are cautiously coming back into place."[3]

CANN IN COURT

Kid Cann's trial began in January 1936. The prosecution kept one eyewitness under police protection and did not even disclose the existence of a third witness who identified Cann as the killer. The witnesses all came forward to tell their story, of seeing Cann fire the gun. Edith Liggett described his "grinning face." She also caused a stir when she said that there had to be a connection between Governor Olson and the killing. Edith shared her husband's political views and crusading spirit. "The murder," she said, "would not have been committed without Governor Olson's permission."[4]

For his part, Kid Cann was cool in the courtroom, at times chewing gum. When he took to the stand in February, he gave the alibi he had professed all along: At the time of the murder, he was in a barbershop. The defense called witnesses to corroborate this testimony, as well as four police officers who contradicted some of Mrs. Liggett's description of the murder scene. Press reports noted that the officers' statements on the stand did not jibe with their earlier police reports.

On February 18, the jury reached its verdict and found Cann not guilty. He was free to continue his life as a "liquor salesman," as he was identified during the trial. Cann would continue to avoid serving any prison time until 1961, when he was convicted of violating the Mann Act as well as bribing a juror. He was released in 1964 and lived another 17 years, spending some of that time in Florida. Land deals there and his other activities enabled him to leave an estate worth $10 million.

Walter Liggett

After the acquittal, Governor Olson said state law enforcement officials "would not rest" until the killers were caught.[5] But no one was ever convicted for the murder of Walter Liggett. His daughter Marda, who saw her father's killing, wrote a detailed account of her father's life and death in 1998. She remained convinced that Cann—or someone who looked like him—had carried out the murder.

THE END OF THE OLD WAYS

What made the O'Connor System, that cozy arrangement between cops and crooks, thrive in St. Paul? Money of course, and specifically, the corrupt cops who would ignore the law for their own gain. That corruption, however, took a big hit in 1935, when Public Safety Commissioner H. E. Warren and the *St. Paul Daily News* joined forces to fight it. Investigators wiretapped the police department's phones and soon recorded several thousand phone calls, many of them offering evidence of corruption. In the fallout of the scandal, thirteen officers were suspended or fired, and the chief of police was also pushed from office. By the next year, reforms were put in place to make sure the O'Connor System would never return.

St. Paul Police Chief John O'Connor

DEATH BY POISON

For widow Della True, a life dominated by poverty and the demands of raising six children proved too much to bear. Early in 1943, she gave her nine-year-old son some milk that contained poison. The boy's unexpected death might not have raised suspicions, except that his six-year-old sister had died the previous October. Under questioning, Della admitted that she had poisoned her children because she couldn't stand the taunts they had to bear because of the family's poverty. A court-ordered exhumation and examination of the girl's body corroborated the mother's confession. While follow-up details of the crime are sketchy, it seems Della served time at the women's prison in Shakopee.

The Post-War Era to the Dawn of the New Millennium

Robbery Leads to Murder 87

The Dentist Did It. 92

The Family That Slays Together . . .99

This Gun For Hire. 104

One Mother's Cruelty, Another's Love 112

Racial Tensions of the Times . . . 119

Paying a High Price 123

A Murder in the Family. 128

Obsession Turns Violent 135

Murder on the Farm 142

A Mystery Resolved 150

The Angry Heir 154

A Cold Case of Murder 161

Robbery Leads to Murder

THE CRIME: A robber-turned-murderer is himself gunned down

PERPETRATOR: Oliver Crutcher

VICTIM: Allan Lee

SCENE OF THE CRIME: St. Paul

WHEN: September 10, 1949

A diagram of the chase route

In the days before reality cop shows, the spectacle of actual crimes being committed stirred the curiosity of some Americans. And for one wild and violent Saturday, the streets of St. Paul were filled with enough police activity and gunfire to attract the attention of thousands of residents. What started as a simple robbery turned into a manhunt that left both a police officer and the criminal dead, another cop wounded, and put one news photographer in harm's way.

ON THE CASE

The day's events started around 4 p.m., when Oliver Crutcher walked into Janssen's Liquor Store on University Avenue. Crutcher, 30 years old, had a long rap sheet, starting more than ten years earlier in his home state of Kentucky. He had twice been convicted of stealing a car and then was nabbed for burglary. Crutcher headed to Indiana, where he had several more arrests, before coming to Minnesota. There, he was arrested twice for assault but got off when the complainant failed to show up in court. Now, in the liquor store, Crutcher was looking for some fast cash.

He handed the clerk $2 and asked for a bottle of whiskey. Then Crutcher pulled out a gun and demanded the money in the cash register. As he fled, a patrol car just happened to be driving by. The two officers inside heard a woman on the street yell, "Stop that man! He just robbed someone."[1]

The police car tailed Crutcher for a bit, then pulled over. Rowan drew his gun and told Crutcher to put his hands up. The officers could see cash jammed into one of his pockets. Crutcher, though, instead of obeying the order, drew his gun and fired. Crutcher seemed to be using blanks, since none of his shots hit the car. Rowan then jumped out of the car and fired his gun as he chased the robber. Crutcher fled down Rondo Avenue, beginning a cat-and-mouse game that would turn fatal.

THE HUNT IS ON

Acting on a tip from a bystander, Rohan, Fahey, and a growing number of officers converged on a house on Rondo. About half-a-dozen officers went inside, thinking they had Crutcher trapped. In the confusion inside, a gun went off, and Officer Odean Jackson was wounded—apparently from a bullet from a fellow officer's gun. Whatever happened, Crutcher was not in the house, and the hunt continued.

At some point during the search, Crutcher was able to elude police and go back to his apartment, where he armed himself with real bullets. Then, for some reason, he returned to the area of the manhunt and entered a home on St. Anthony Avenue. Acting on another tip, police went to the front door of the house. Detectives Allan Lee and William Crowell walked onto the porch with their guns drawn. In the rear of the house, police questioned a woman who lived there.

Hi Paul, a photographer for the *St. Paul Pioneer Press*, had arrived with the cops. One of them told him to go around the front and talk to Lee, to tell him to check if there was a basement window at the front of the house. Paul found Lee and went to look for the window himself, since the detective didn't want to leave his post. Paul described for *Pioneer Press* readers what happened next: "I walked about 10 feet to the edge of the porch and was just bending over to look when I heard a BANG and saw a blinding flash from the corner

MINNEAPOLIS TRIBUNE PHOTO BY POWELL KRUEGER

SLAIN DETECTIVE'S PARTNER DRAWS GUN FOR REVENGE ON KILLER
Detective Bill Crowley, right, and patrolman Bill Henry, stalk gunman outside St. Paul apartment house

Detective William Crowley draws his gun in the hunt for Oliver Crutcher, who had just killed Crowley's partner

of my eye. Four other shots followed in quick succession, and everybody in the vicinity fell to the ground . . . I saw a dark form hurdle off the porch and run down the street. Unthinking, I started to run after him."[2]

Paul then heard someone call out that a detective had been shot. He realized that it must have been Lee, and the hurdling form was the fugitive Crutcher. Lee died shortly after he reached the hospital.

With a fellow officer down, the hunt intensified. The police presence grew to some 50 men, and they began searching house to house on Rondo Avenue, sometimes knocking down doors to investigate who was inside. As darkness set in, the fire department brought in huge floodlights. Police lines held back a crowd that grew to about 3,000 people. Finally around 10:15, the police seemed to have Crutcher cornered in a second-flood apartment at 227 Rondo. They fired tear gas into the building, then asked for volunteer officers to don gas masks and search inside.

One officer who responded was Jim Griffin. He had been off-duty when he heard about the situation on Rondo and headed over to help. Going up the stairs to pursue Crutcher, he later recalled, "I was scared to death and could hardly breathe."[3] Joining him was John Mercado. As he entered the room where Crutcher was thought to be, Mercado saw an elbow sticking out from under the bed. He signaled to other the officers that they had found their man. Without hesitation, the officers opened fire. Press reports made it sound like Crutcher confronted the cops, but he never said a word or fired a shot. The killing of Crutcher, an African-American man, caused a great deal of controversy in the African-American community.

Police believed that Crutcher was part of a small gang that had committed several recent hold-ups. Several lived on Rondo Avenue, which probably explained why Crutcher fled there. One of the members of the gang was Crutcher's wife. Whatever crimes they had committed together before, Oliver Crutcher had decided to go solo that September day, sparking the series of events that led to the first killing of a St. Paul police officer in 15 years and his own bloody death. In 2000, the city of St. Paul honored officers Griffin, Mercado, and a third officer who entered the Rondo Avenue apartment with them, Vernon Michel. The men received the Medal of Valor for volunteering to face what could have been their own demise.

FROM CHEATING TO MURDER

At work, Arthur DeZeler was a valuable employee. At home, though, DeZeler was something of a philanderer, as at least two of his three wives knew it. Grace, the third, had gotten involved with him while she was still married to her previous husband. By 1947, their six-year marriage was on the rocks, and Grace planned to file for divorce. Before she could, she disappeared, and Arthur was a suspect. Finally, several weeks after her disappearance, Grace's body floated to the surface of Little Bass Lake near Cohasset. Her killer had tried to keep her at the bottom of the lake by tying the body to a concrete block. An autopsy revealed that she had died from a blow to the head. Once again, police zeroed in on Mr. DeZeler. In court, his lawyers tried to paint Grace as a loose woman, who may have been trying to abort a baby—not Arthur's—at the time of her death. Arthur's philandering lifestyle also emerged during the trial. In the end, the evidence against DeZeler led to his conviction and a life sentence.

Grace DeZeler's death certificate

The Dentist Did it

THE CRIME: A Minneapolis dentist sedates and sexually assaults his female patients, eventually leading to murder

PERPETRATOR: Dr. A. Arnold Axilrod

VICTIM: Mary Moonen

SCENE OF THE CRIME: Body discovered on Thomas Avenue South, Minneapolis

WHEN: April 23, 1955

Minneapolis Morning Tribune

Dr. A. Arnold Axilrod

On a regular basis, we put our trust—perhaps even our lives—in the hands of trained professionals. We count on them to do their jobs at least competently, if not always expertly. Mary Moonen probably had that faith in 1955 when she first visited the office of A. Arnold Axilrod, a Minneapolis dentist who'd been practicing for almost 20 years. A slight man with a mustache and a penchant for smoking pipes, Axilrod probably came across as a mild and soothing figure to his patients. But he had a reputation as a ladies' man, and many of his female clients came from the Hoop De Do, a nightclub located below his office. The locale above the club didn't seem to bother Moonen, though her trips to the dentist soon created problems that went far beyond her teeth.

Moonen made her first appointment early in 1955, at the suggestion of her sister Janice Newton, who lived in Minneapolis. Moonen was new to the city, having moved there from Plummer, Minnesota, where she had briefly lived on her in-laws' farm. Moonen, née Frederickson, had married Mathias Moonen in 1953. Shortly after their nuptials, Mathias was drafted and in the spring of 1954 found himself serving in South Korea. Several months later, Mary had a baby, and she decided to move with the child to Minneapolis to live with her father.

DR. AXILROD'S METHODS

Mary Moonen's first visit to Dr. Axilrod didn't seem to be out of the ordinary. But during her second or third appointment, the doctor decided she needed more serious treatment—serious enough for him to administer a sedative mixture of his own concoction. In a capsule, he combined Seconal and Nembutal, two barbiturates, with Anacin, an over-the-counter drug that combines aspirin with caffeine. As Axilrod later explained, "The capsule was not intended to put the patient to sleep; it was merely to slow down reflexes. Some patients get pretty jumpy when you start to drill."[1] For Moonen and others, the mixture left them semiconscious for hours.

With Moonen's first dose, the drugged state lasted about four hours. The dentist offered to drive her home after; Mr. Frederickson's apartment was not far from his office. Moonen accepted the gesture, and arrived home showing the effects of the sedative. Her father recalled that she looked "very pale, her eyes were blurry, and she was very nervous."[2] After a second visit a few weeks later that once again required the sedative, Moonen came home in even worse shape. Once again, Axilrod had escorted her to the apartment.

A few months after the trips to Axilrod's office began, Mary Moonen discovered she was pregnant. Her suspicions immediately turned to Axilrod and his potent pills. She said as much to her doctor, Glen Peterson, saying Axilrod was the likely father. Still, even with her hunch about Axilrod's treachery, she made arrangements to see him again at his office, on the night of April 22. There, she accused him of fathering the baby she was carrying. Axilrod suggested the two go for a ride to discuss the situation, and Moonen agreed.

According to Axilrod, as they drove, Moonen said she would expose his crimes to the world. Moonen might not have been in that position at all, driving with the man she was threatening to expose for rape, if another woman had taken steps months before. At the end of 1954, Minneapolis police received a call from a young woman who accused Axilrod of drugging and raping her. The woman, though, refused to give her name and didn't want to press charges, so the police let the matter drop. But Moonen, violated and angry, was ready to act.

So was Axilrod. He later told police the accusations from Moonen left him "boiling mad," but then he blacked out.[3] He didn't know where or when he lost consciousness, but he did know that when he came to, Moonen was no longer in the car.

GETTING THE FACTS

Saturday morning, April 23, as John J. Cowles Jr. backed his Pontiac out of its garage, he saw something odd in an alley nearby. Cowles was a journalist, and his family owned all of the major Minneapolis papers. He went over to investigate, and what at first looked like merely a pile of clothing was the dead body of Mary Moonen. An autopsy later confirmed what marks on Moonen's throat suggested—she had been strangled. The examination also revealed the fetus Moonen was carrying, as well as signs of recent sexual intercourse.

A Famous Coroner

Leading the autopsy of Mary Moonen was Dr. John Coe, chief of pathology at what was then called Minneapolis General Hospital (today's Hennepin County Medical Center). Coe saw damage to the brain and lungs that suggested the murder was a strangulation, and the marks outside Moonen's throat and signs of bleeding inside confirmed it. During his long career in medicine, Coe made a name for himself in the world of pathology, and he credited the Axilrod case with boosting his desire to learn more about forensic medicine. His greatest achievement was developing a method for determining time of death after rigor mortis had ended. Coe learned that levels of potassium found in eyeball fluid increase as more time passes. Measuring those potassium levels can help coroners pin down the time of death.

The clues found on Moonen's body included a prescription written by her doctor. Police visited Peterson, who relayed what Moonen had told him about her encounters with Axilrod. The police immediately went to the dentist's office to bring him in for questioning (though they let him first finish up on a patient). At the station, Axilrod appeared nervous, and at first denied having seen Moonen the night before. Then, wringing his hands, he admitted he had worked on Moonen's teeth that evening, then the two went for a drive. He also described the allegations Moonen made about him and his rising anger. The dentist denied that he was the father of Moonen's baby, though the two did have sex that night. Then, Axilrod told the police about his blacking out, and that when he awoke, "I knew that all at once she was no longer there."[4]

Minneapolis Morning Tribune

Mary Moonen and her husband

Axilrod regained his consciousness, he said, while driving his car—not far from the site where Moonen lay dead. As Axilrod finished his story, one of the detectives posed a hypothetical: What would Axilrod say if he learned that Moonen had been strangled? "If the pathologist said she was strangled," Axilrod replied, "it must have been me. There was nobody else there."[5] Despite those statements, Axilrod did not sign a confession. The police, though, did hold him without charge and the Hennepin County attorney soon made plans for a grand jury inquiry.

The Minneapolis police began questioning some of Axilrod's female patients, including the dead woman's sister. Janice Newton said that on her most recent visit, which began at 4:30 p.m., she didn't leave the dentist's office until 11 that night. At that point, she said, she was groggy, and the mental fog lasted for about two days. Newton believed she had been drugged.

On April 26, the *Minneapolis Tribune* reported that police had found several other women who complained of strangely long sessions in Axilrod's office. The most startling story came from a 17-year-old, who had seen the dentist in April. She arrived for a 6 p.m. appointment and didn't leave until 1 a.m., with Axilrod bringing her home. The girl or her mother—sources vary—called police to report the incident, as the girl "thought it funny" she had been sedated for so long.[6] The girl, though, did not want to come down to the station and press charges, much like the anonymous caller to the police a few months earlier. In this case, though, there was no claim of sexual molestation. To the local press, Axilrod explained the incident by saying the teen had gotten sleepy from the sedative, and he had trouble waking her. He "just thought it best to let her sleep it off."[7]

As the women stepped forward to speak out about Axilrod's unorthodox dentistry, his wife Fanny publicly supported her husband. "My husband couldn't have done it," she said. "I'm with my husband all the way and so are our family and friends."[8] After police formally charged Axilrod, his wife came to visit him at the police station. Detective captain Eugene Bernath watched as Fanny asked her husband if he would swear that the baby Moonen had been carrying was not his. As the detective later recounted, the dentist said "By God I swear," and his wife replied, "By God I believe you."[9] But Axilrod's possible role in the Moonen killing went unmentioned.

ON TRIAL

In May, Axilrod was indicted for first-degree murder. Leading his defense was Sydney Goff, a St. Paul attorney. As a lawyer, he had won an acquittal in an earlier, well-publicized murder case. Goff hired private detectives to try to track down the "real" killer and helped orchestrate a public relations campaign that tried to paint Axilrod as a responsible family man incapable of murder. Goff managed to win a delay of the trial until September. As the trial date approached, interest in the case ran high in the Twin Cities, and a local TV station sought permission to broadcast it, but was turned down.

The trial kicked off on September 19, with an initial pool of about 200 potential jurors called to the Hennepin County Courthouse. The selection process went slowly, and in the meantime, a witness subpoenaed by the defense stirred up more interest in the case. The witness was Donald Newton, Mary

The Hennepin County Courthouse

Moonen's brother-in-law, and a recent widower, as Janice Newton had died over the summer from a skin-related disease. Newton had an extensive criminal record, and some people theorized that Goff might be trying to make him a prime suspect in the Moonen killing. Newton caused a stir when he claimed that the private detectives who subpoenaed him also tried to bribe him, which they denied. When Newton's accusation made the newspaper. Goff called for a change of venue and a mistrial. The presiding judge, Leslie Anderson, denied both motions.

Jury selection went on until October 6. Meanwhile, Donald Newton had become news again, as the defense presented what it said were sworn statements from two criminals who claimed Newton had earlier told them he had slept with his sister-in-law. They also claimed that Newton said his earlier claim of bribery had been cooked up by the prosecution. Goff filed a motion, based on the new "evidence," that would allow both the defense and prosecution to cross examine Newton on the stand. Once again, Anderson denied the motion

The Brother-in-Law

Donald Newton's long history of criminal activity before the Axilrod trial included robbery, forgery and car theft. As the trial was getting underway. Newton was out on bail for an alleged burglary, and on September 19 he added a charge of indecent exposure to his rap sheet. He pleaded guilty and was sentenced to 90 days in the county workhouse. That December, Newton found himself in Stillwater State Prison. Because of three felony convictions and breaking the terms of his probation, he was sentenced to a life term as a habitual criminal.

The state's case rested primarily on the testimony of the Minneapolis detectives who had first questioned Axilrod and heard his statements about what happened the night of April 22. For the defense, Goff did not call Axilrod to testify on his own behalf, but Fanny Axilrod did appear. Along with singing her husband's praises, she said he had arrived home just after midnight on the 22nd. The prosecution had not definitely established that Moonen died before then, creating some doubt about Axilrod's guilt. Goff also added a new wrinkle when he called taxi driver Leonard Ugland to the stand. The cabbie said he saw Moonen and Axilrod arguing in parked car. Moonen exited the car, Axilrod drove off, and the young woman then entered another car with two men in it. The story seemed conveniently beneficial to the defense, especially coming at the last minute. The prosecution then presented three rebuttal witnesses, who, as the Associated Press reported, basically echoed this sentiment: "Ugland's reputation for truthfulness [was] 'bad' and [they] would not believe the man under oath."[10]

THE COURTS SPEAK

In his closing statement, Goff portrayed the case against Axilrod as an attempt by a lazy police force to railroad an innocent man. When the jury left for deliberations, it had a range of charges to consider, not just the first-degree murder charge that Axilrod initially faced. Judge Anderson said the jurors could also find him guilty on lesser charges, and that's what they did, returning a verdict of guilty of first-degree manslaughter. In a final statement before the court, Axilrod proclaimed his innocence, asserting, "Since I was a young child . . . I never deliberately hurt anyone in my life."[11] Axilrod walked out of court facing a sentence of 5 to 20 years.

He managed to stay out of jail for a time, though, as Goff's appeal worked its way through the state Supreme Court. That court upheld the verdict the next spring. At Stillwater State Prison, Axilrod sought parole several times before finally winning his release in 1964. His health frail, he went to Ohio, where, as Fanny Axilrod said, "I've made a life for us and we just want to live it." The faithful wife also restated her belief in her husband's innocence, saying, "He was convicted on adverse publicity, but I would rather not go into that."[12]

The Family That Slays Together

THE CRIME: Three brothers go on a crime spree that includes robbery, killing a police officer and kidnapping, launching a massive manhunt

PERPETRATORS: James, Roger and Ronald O'Kasick

SCENE OF THE CRIME: Minneapolis and Anoka County

WHEN: August 17, 1957, through September 14, 1957

Minneapolis Morning Tribune

ROGER O'KASICK   RONALD O'KASICK

Two of the O'Kasick brothers

In the debate over nature versus nurture and determining whether someone is likely to turn to a life of crime, recent studies have placed more of an emphasis on genes. There's no question that crime seemed to run in the O'Kasick family of Minneapolis. Yet the home environment that shaped brothers Roger, Ronald and James certainly wasn't a plus. An abusive father, a life of poverty, a mother who died when James, the youngest of the three, was just 14—these factors didn't help the brothers as their characters were shaped. In the end, the three perpetrators of one of Minnesota's most sensational crime sprees all died violently before they passed through their 20s.

And they weren't even the only O'Kasick children who turned to crime. Older brother Richard had spent time in the St. Cloud Reformatory for several robberies, while sister Joyce served time for forgery—only to escape during her sentence. It wasn't a daring prison break; Joyce simply walked away from the women's reformatory in Shakopee, in the midst of the 1957 manhunt for Roger, Ronald and Jimmy. She had a feeling, she told newspapers, that something bad was going to happen to them—a logical guess, given their track record.

POLICE CONFRONTATION

By August 16, 1957, Ronald and Roger had already been committing robberies for several years. Jimmy had joined the crime family that spring, after his discharge from the Marines, helping his brothers rob several pharmacies that summer. On the night of the 16th, they stole a car and customized it with a metal plate that they could pull down over the back window to deflect bullets from police.

The next night, the O'Kasicks were on their way to rob another store when they noticed a police cruiser. They put the stolen car into a U-turn and the police began to give chase. In the patrol car were officers Robert Fossum and Ward Canfield. The cops pursued the brothers down Blaisdell Avenue to 39th Street, where the stolen car began to skid. Roger, behind the wheel, lost control and smashed into a parked car. The bumpers of the two cars hooked together, and the O'Kasicks' car spun into the street. The patrol car soon reached the scene and it too lost control and came to a stop. The officers and the O'Kasicks all jumped out of their cars and began a gun battle in the street. Like the gangsters of the 1930s, the crooks outgunned their opponents, brandishing high-powered rifles and firing armor-piercing bullets.

Killed in the Line of Duty

Officer Robert Fossum

When the shooting stopped, Fossum was dead from a bullet to the head, and Canfield was wounded in the hip, shot by James. The O'Kasicks jumped back into their car, which was still hitched to the parked vehicle they had hit. As they drove off, they caught Canfield's body under their car and dragged him down the street. After about 20 feet, the officer's body finally came loose. He would eventually have his right leg amputated.

TAKING FLIGHT

Abandoning their car on Van Nest Street, the brothers carjacked two different vehicles as they made their getaway. With the second vehicle, they briefly took the passenger as a hostage, before pushing her out in a south Minneapolis alley. The O'Kasicks abandoned that car and then set off on foot before finally stealing a 1950 Olds. A huge manhunt began for the trio, which the brothers avoided by eventually staying in Superior National Forest and then the woods near Forest Lake, sleeping on the ground.

On September 14, in Anoka County, two police officers spotted a young man walking down the road with a gas can. It was Ronald O'Kasick. The officers offered him a ride to his car, and Ronald accepted. When they stopped by the car Ronald claimed was his, the actual owner came out and began yelling at Ronald. At this point the officers handcuffed Ronald.

Jimmy and Roger observed all this, and they advanced on the police car with guns drawn. In the shootout that followed, one officer was wounded, and Ronald managed to join his brothers. Meanwhile a local resident, Eugene Lindgren, had heard the gunfire and went to get his own gun. As he reached his garage, he came upon the O'Kasicks. The three forced Lindgren to take them away from the scene in his Cadillac.

During the gun battle, one of the officers had managed to enter a home and call for help. The radio calls that went out drew several hundred police officers to the back roads of Columbus Township, where they pursued the stolen Cadillac. The O'Kasicks and Lindgren ended up in Carlos Avery Game Refuge, where their car slid off a dirt road into a swamp. The brothers then forced Lindgren to flee with them on foot. Overhead, a state patrol plane pinpointed the fugitives and radioed the pursuing officers. One got as close as 25 feet away from the O'Kasicks, but he feared hitting Lindgren so he held his fire.

The officer needn't have worried. Just as Lindgren called out, "Don't shoot or they will kill me," Roger put a gun to the man's head and fired.[1] Roger had been the one who killed Fossum at close range too. After the shot, Officer James Crawford told the men to surrender. The O'Kasicks refused, so Crawford fired two rounds from his shotgun into the thicket that screened them from view. When the police went to investigate, they found the dead bodies of Ronald and Roger O'Kasick. A sudden shot startled the officers, who then found the bleeding body of Jimmy. He had tried to kill himself, but failed.

Taken back to Minneapolis, the wounded brother gave police details of the crime spree that started with the summer robberies and ended with the shootings in Anoka County. The brothers' father, Michael, tearfully told reporters "I never thought they would do anything like that. It just isn't like them."[2] The elder O'Kasick's comments came shortly after he had been arrested in Duluth for violating parole. He'd earlier been in the state prison serving time for robbery.

The next year, James was tried and convicted of murder. While at the St. Cloud Reformatory, on the anniversary of the second shootout, Jimmy wrote his older brother Richard a note—a suicide note. With a knife he had stolen from the dining hall, Jimmy successfully did what he had failed to do in that Anoka County swamp. Richard, for his part, had given up crime by then. He later changed his last name so he wouldn't be associated with his notorious brothers. But he also claimed that one of the crimes laid at his brothers' feet—the slaying of Eugene Lindgren—was a bum rap. He said Jimmy had told him the police had killed the hostage and tried to cover it up. But the police and the courts stuck to the story that Roger O'Kasick committed that last act of violence before he was gunned down.

The St. Cloud Reformatory

FAMILY KILLING

On a Thursday night in 1957, 33-year-old Douglas Person attended a community dinner with his family in the rural town of Shafer. He was friendly to everyone there, including his parents Emory and Mabel and his sister Lois. But by the next morning, the three family members were dead, victims of a murderous rampage that Person could not remember. Later though, the details emerged: he bludgeoned his father with a hammer and a splitting maul in the basement, then headed upstairs to kill his sister and mother with the hammer. Seeing her crazed son approaching with the weapon, Mabel ripped a latch off a screen door in a futile effort to escape. Lois was found on the stairs leading to the second floor, wearing her pajamas. Person, a former serviceman, had experienced psychological problems before, leading to shock treatments. Realizing the horrible deed he'd committed, he went to a neighbor's house and tearfully confessed his crime. Hearing that a doctor was on his way, Person pleaded not to let the man hurt him. Ironically, his family had bought the farm in Shafer thinking life in the country would do their troubled son good.

This Gun for Hire

The Thompson home

THE CRIME: A husband arranges the murder of his wife, seeking a huge life insurance payout

PERPETRATORS: T. Eugene Thompson, murderer Dick W. C. Anderson, and "go-between" Norman Mastrian

VICTIM: Carol Thompson

SCENE OF THE CRIME: 1720 Hillcrest Avenue, St. Paul

WHEN: March 6, 1963

The classic 1940s film noir *Double Indemnity* has it all: illicit love, a murder plot to secure cash and remove a marital obstruction, and a dogged investigator determined to find the truth about what looks like a random, accidental death. But the movie, and the book it's based on, is fiction. The Carol Thompson story is a real-life variation of *Double Indemnity* that shocked the country.

To outsiders, it might have seemed that Carol and her family were living the American dream in their suburban slice of St. Paul. Their house on Hillcrest Avenue was flanked by other two- and three-story homes with a Tudor feel, all finely landscaped. Carol was well liked by everyone who knew her. They admired her skills at knitting and bridge and her curiosity about the world. Her husband, T. Eugene Thompson, was a successful St. Paul lawyer. "Cotton," as he was known, chaired a committee of the Minnesota Bar Association and had served as a trustee of his church. The couple had four children, one boy and three girls. The eldest, Jeff, attended a private school near the family's home. But as is often the case, behind the façade of domestic tranquility was a life that others didn't know about—until T. Eugene Thompson's true feelings and actions came out in court.

A MURDER GONE WRONG

The morning of March 6, 1963, saw some minor variations in the routines of the Thompson household. Mr. Thompson usually left fairly late, reaching his office around 10:30 a.m. That day, though, he left before 8:00, and he offered Jeff a ride to school. The boy, who usually walked, accepted the ride.

Shortly after reaching his office, Thompson asked his secretary to ring his house—another slight departure from his routine, but Thompson wanted to assure Carol that he would be free that night to watch the kids while she took a class. As Carol came down the stairs from the second floor to answer the phone, she didn't know that someone was waiting for her in the basement.

The man listened for the sound of Mrs. Thompson heading back upstairs, then made his way out of the basement. He found her in a bedroom. The intruder demanded that the woman turn away from him, lie face down on the bed, and tell him where the family kept its valuables. Carol complied, only to receive a blow to the back of the head that knocked her out. The criminal had hit her with a thick rubber hose. Then he undressed her and carried her to the bathroom, where a waiting tub was filled with water.

The robber was actually a murderer, and his plan was to drown Carol in the bathtub. The plan went awry, however, when the victim regained consciousness and scrambled out of the tub. As she ran down the hall, the killer pulled out a gun, but it misfired, giving Carol a chance to get down the stairs and reach the front door. The door, though, was secured by a chain, and before she could undo it, the intruder hit her in the head with his gun. Carol tried to buy her way to safety. "Here, take this," she said, offering the man her diamond ring. He took it, then brought down his gun again against her skull. "Oh, God," Carol moaned. "Help me."[1]

The job still not done, the killer went into the kitchen and returned with a paring knife. He slashed and stabbed Mrs. Thompson repeatedly, until the blade broke off in her neck. Thinking his victim was finally dead, the murderer went back upstairs to create the believable aftermath of a robbery. After a few moments, he heard the sound of a door opening. Carol had survived the attack and was now on her way for help. Instead of pursuing her outside, the man left the house and went home to get rid of his bloody clothes and his gun.

MURDER ROCKS SUBURBIA

Sometime during her ordeal, Carol Thompson had managed to grab a light robe. Bleeding from the neck and head, she staggered from one neighbor's house to another, until Mrs. Ruth Nelson finally opened her door. She was stunned to see a lightly clad, barefoot woman in the snow, covered in blood. Nelson and several family members helped Carol into their home, and soon another neighbor appeared—Dr. Fritz Pearson, whose wife had seen Thompson's bloody state. The doctor wiped away the blood; the police and an ambulance soon arrived. Carol, not fully conscious, could not say who had attacked her.

A map showing the location of the scene of the crime

Around 9:15, the phone rang in T. Eugene Thompson's law office. It was one of the Nelsons, calling to tell the lawyer about the brutal attack on his wife. After a brief stop at the Nelson home, Thompson went to the hospital, where his wife's condition was deteriorating. A team of medical experts tried to maintain her heartbeat and keep her breathing, but they failed. Shortly before 1 p.m., Carol Thompson died.

At the hospital, police briefly questioned Mr. Thompson. He wondered if burglary had been the perpetrator's motive, and the ransacked bedroom the police found at 1720 Hillcrest seemed to support that conclusion. Thompson also speculated that perhaps one of the criminals he had once represented targeted his wife, an idea the newspapers later picked up.

As the police investigation began, word spread quickly through the Twin Cities about the brazen daytime home invasion and murder. A crime like that, as journalist William Swanson notes in his book *Dial M: The Murder of Carol Thompson*, was "especially freakish in Highland Park, a stable, upper-middle-class corner of the city where police were rarely called except for an occasional bicycle theft or loud car."[2] A journalist of the era, Donald John Giese, summed up the tense atmosphere of the day, as spouses called each other to check in, and women who were home alone refused to open their doors for strangers. Meanwhile, a constant parade of cars slowly streamed by the Thompson house, curious about such a macabre crime.

A SECRET LIFE

The police investigation entailed questioning the Thompsons' social circle. Everyone agreed on Carol's wonderful qualities. Most also agreed that Cotton was a good provider for his family, though with a streak of arrogance and something of a wandering eye when it came to women. But the common sentiment was that Thompson wouldn't cheat on his wife. Common sentiment, though, was very wrong.

Almost three years earlier, during the course of his practice, Thompson had established a professional relationship with Jacqueline Okoneski, who had come to his office seeking a divorce. The professional turned personal, as the lawyer and the client began a relationship that continued even after Okoneski remarried and became Jackie Olesen.

Thompson's relationship with Olesen had many facets. There was a sexual aspect, as they spent time together in Chicago and at the Thompsons' lake-side cottage in Minnesota. Thompson also loaned his mistress money so she could go to business school, then she repaid him when she began working in his firm, though by January 1962 she had left the job as her relationship with Ronald Olesen deepened. Around this time, in February, Thompson begged

Okoneski to hold off on marrying Olesen. "Just give me a year."[3] In that time, the lawyer said, he could secure enough money to support both his lover and his family. Okoneski refused.

Her new marriage, however, was stormy, and by the summer of 1962 Jackie Olesen was back in Thompson's office as a client, seeking another divorce. As that process played out, Thompson tried to wheedle his way back into Olesen's emotional life, offering her money and an apartment if they could be a couple again. Olesen turned him down.

As Thompson thought of ways to increase his finances and share the wealth with Jackie, he and Carol began to talk about life insurance. If Cotton died first, his life insurance and the expected inheritance from Carol's father, a successful plumber, would total about $1 million. Thompson reasoned that taking out policies of about that value on Carol made sense, in case she died first. To apply for the life insurance policies, Eugene gave Carol several forms to sign. The amounts of the policies, though, were left blank.

As the investigation of Carol Thompson's murder continued, the large life insurance polices taken out in her name, which included double-indemnity provisions, intrigued insurance investigator Joe Healy. The fact that Thompson had much more coverage for his wife than himself was out of the ordinary. Digging deeper, Healy learned about little things Thompson had done before March 1963 that seemed odd. For one, he gave away the family pet, a dachshund prone to making noise. Thompson also removed the extension phone from the second floor of the house, so if someone—say, Carol—were alone upstairs and the phone rang, she would have to go downstairs. Healy also learned about the changes to his routine that Thompson made on the morning of March 6. "After a couple of days' checking," Healy later said, ". . . I decided that the husband was as good a suspect as any."[4]

The St. Paul police agreed. They had received tips about Thompson's philandering ways from several sources and interviewed Jackie Olesen about her relationship with Thompson. She freely offered details of their affair. But Thompson's straying and the large insurance policies were no smoking gun. It took several more months for the state to label the bereaved widower the prime suspect.

PLOTTING MURDER

By April, T. Eugene Thompson had mostly resumed a normal life, though he had given up his office and now worked at home. The police, taking a new tack, showed the public some of the items that the killer had left behind at the scene of the crime. These included the broken pistol grip of a Luger. The grip had been hand-made, and its creator recognized it. The gun had been stolen from his house several weeks before Carol Thompson was killed.

Minneapolis Morning Tribune

Carol Thompson

Another clue came when police arrested petty crooks Willard Ingram and Henry Butler, who confessed to stealing the Luger and to several other crimes. The gun, Ingram explained, had ended up with Norman Mastrian—a former boxer and classmate of Thompson's in college who happened to have become one of his clients during the summer of 1962. Butler then said he had seen Mastrian give the gun to Dick W. C. Anderson, a former Marine, now a roofing salesman.

Anderson was the last of several men Mastrian approached with a proposition: use the Luger to kill a suburban housewife and mother of four, in return for $2,000. Ingram, Butler, and a third criminal named Richard Sharp all turned him down, but Anderson was game.

With this information, police tracked down Anderson in Phoenix, where he claimed to be on vacation. Confronted with the outline of a plot he knew to be true—the murder-for-hire plot with Mastrian, the jammed gun, the beating and slashing of Carol Thompson—Anderson admitted his guilt. "What kind of deal can I get if I go back there and cooperate with you people?" the accused murderer asked.[5] He was told, no deals.

The police had already picked up Mastrian in St. Paul, and the two were soon indicted for murder. While behind bars, Anderson came forward to tell everything he knew about the murder plot—including the actions Thompson took to make the killing happen. These included leaving the side door that Anderson used to enter the house unlocked and calling Carol that morning, so she would have to answer the only phone, on the first floor. Almost immediately, Thompson found himself under arrest for first-degree murder.

IN COURT

In the months leading up to his trial, T. Eugene Thompson proclaimed his innocence. But as the case unfolded in late October and November 1963, the circumstantial evidence seemed to grow. Thompson tried to parry the prosecutorial thrusts: Why did he get rid of the dog known to bark at strangers? Well, the Thompsons had just installed new carpeting and the dog was staining it. Getting rid of the upstairs phone? Part of a plan to coordinate the phone's color with redecorating that had gone on there. The jurors heard all this, as well as testimony from Jackie Olesen and about Mastrian's failed efforts to procure a killer before finding Dick Anderson, and Anderson's description of the botched murder. And they saw Thompson weep openly as he absorbed Anderson's testimony.

Thompson took the stand in his own defense, and he testified that he told Carol about his affair with Jackie Olesen. He claimed that she said she already knew about it. He denied telling Olesen that he wanted more time to straighten out his finances so he could be with her. And while he acknowledged knowing Norman Mastrian, Thompson flatly said he had not used him as a middleman to arrange his wife's killing. Money he had given Mastrian—$2,500—was repayment of an unused retainer Mastrian had given him earlier.

In the closing statements, defense attorney Hyam Segell admitted his client was not a man that everyone liked. But he was also not the monster who arranged for his wife to be murdered. The jury, though, disagreed. After deliberating for about 26 hours, it found T. Eugene Thompson guilty. *The New York Times* reported how Thompson "stared intently at each juror as the court clerk polled the panel."[6] After the announcement of the verdict, Thompson was sentenced to life in prison.

The Thompson case took another turn the next summer, when Dick Anderson recanted much of his testimony that fingered Mastrian and Thompson as the plotters of Carol Thompson's death. The Minnesota Supreme Court directed the trial court to consider whether Anderson's recantation had any merit. Back in court and under oath, Anderson stuck by his original testimony; he recanted, he said, only because of threats directed at him by Mastrian and Thompson, who were all incarcerated at Stillwater State Prison.

Thompson served 20 years of his sentence. Afterward, he still had cordial relations with his children, even though they believed that he had arranged the death of their mother.

A Second Trial

Jeff Thompson, the eldest child in the family, followed in his father's footsteps and became a lawyer. In 1986, three years after his father's release from prison on parole, Jeff suggested that he and his sisters hold a second trial for their father, with Jeff as prosecutor. As Jeff later told a local reporter, "The purpose was for him to prove to us he really had been wrongfully convicted . . . this was going to be his one chance." T. Eugene Thompson, however, could not produce evidence that convinced his children he was not guilty in orchestrating the death of their mother. When asked if it would help him understand or forgive his father if the elder Thompson did admit his guilt, Jeff replied, "I don't know."[7]

One Mother's Cruelty, Another's Love

THE CRIME: A young boy is murdered; after decades, the case is reopened and the murderer finally faces justice

PERPETRATOR: Lois Jurgens

VICTIM: Dennis Craig Jurgens

SCENE OF THE CRIME: White Bear Lake

WHEN: Death occurred around April 11, 1965

The Minneapolis Star & Tribune

Lois Jurgens

A parent's love for a child is usually a given, despite the exasperation young— or even adult—offspring can trigger. But not all mothers feel a maternal bond, and if the parent is mentally unstable, that emotional distance can become more pronounced.

With Lois Jurgens, some emotional imbalance seemed to trigger her violent, even tortuous, outbursts with her adopted children. And for years, no one knew that her actions led to the death of her five-year-old son Dennis— though plenty of people in White Bear Lake had their suspicions.

DIFFICULT TIMES

Dennis had been born on December 6, 1961, to an unwed teenage mother, who put him up for adoption. He was barely a year old when he entered the home of Lois and Harold Jurgens, joining an adopted sibling, Robert. The Jurgens had tried for years to have children of their own; during the mid 1950s, Lois's inability to conceive seemed to cause emotional disturbances that led her to receive shock therapy, among other treatments. In 1960, the couple used an independent agency to adopt Robert. Shortly after, they received the blessing of Ramsey County officials to use the state adoption apparatus, though a county official noted Lois had a tendency to display a "rigid manner and need for perfection."[1] Still, the caseworker believed that Lois wanted to be a good mother.

Despite that appearance, Lois did seem to have some misgivings about Dennis. He was bigger than his new older brother, which bothered her somewhat, and she worried how he would get along with Robert. But Harold Jurgens was thrilled to have a second son in the family.

It didn't take long, however, for Dennis to experience physical trauma that went beyond the usual childhood scrapes and bruises. In August 1963, the Jurgenses took him to the hospital after he was severely burned on his stomach, buttocks and genitals. Lois explained that she had put Dennis in the sink to bathe him and turned on the water at too high a temperature. The doctor who treated Dennis thought the burn area was unusual, but said nothing.

Family members, relatives of Harold's, also later recalled odd behavior from Lois at Dennis's expense. They saw her lift the boy up by the ears or strike him. They saw her force-feed him. They saw Dennis tied to the toilet when Lois wanted him to have a bowel movement. They saw the happy, energetic boy who came to the Jurgens household in 1962 transform into a withdrawn child. But no one expressed their concerns for Dennis's welfare to anyone outside the family.

AN APRIL WEEKEND

On Friday, April 9, 1965, Harold Jurgens, an electrician by trade, drove to northern Wisconsin to do some work in a friend's home. The next day, he received a call from Lois: She and Dennis had "been at it," which Harold knew was not a good thing.[2] He immediately returned home.

The next morning, around 9:30, Lois found Dennis in his crib, obviously in physical distress. The family called the doctor, and Lois said the boy had fallen the day before and had been running a fever. Whatever Dennis's ailment, the doctor could do nothing for him. By 10 a.m., Dennis was dead.

The police were called in to investigate the death. The assistant chief at the time was Lois's brother, Jerome Zerwas; he took himself off the case immediately. Meanwhile, as the investigation went on, the coroner put "deferred" on the death certificate under the cause of death. But he never received any information that led him to change the wording. Dr. Robert Woodburn then performed an autopsy and determined the cause of death was a ruptured bowel that led to peritonitis. Woodburn also noted bruises—dozens of them—across the boy's body. Not all of them would be hidden from mourners when they came to pay their last respects.

County officials soon called a juvenile court hearing to investigate the matter further. About 50 people testified, including relatives. Some of them recounted incidents of abuse they had seen. Carol Felix, a social worker who was later granted access to the hearing's sealed files, said the witnesses provided "details of sadistic behavior on the part of Mrs. Jurgens."[3] The acts, it was later learned, included clipping a clothespin to his penis.

As a result of the hearing, Robert Jurgens was removed from the home. But no charges were brought against Lois Jurgens, and the death certificate continued to read "deferred." And since the testimony taken at the hearing was sealed, people in a position to shape the lives of other children did not hear about Lois's sadistic acts. They didn't see the photos showing Dennis's bruised corpse. So, in 1969, Robert was allowed back into the home. And when doctors examined Lois, they determined she was fit to be an adoptive mother. So fit, that in 1972 four more children came to the Jurgens' home.

MORE TROUBLES

The four kids—three boys and a girl—were siblings from a Kentucky family, the Howtons. By this time, the Jurgens family was living in Stillwater. While the location had changed, Lois's hideous behavior hadn't. The Howtons faced late-night inspections of their rooms, with corporal punishment the penalty for anything Lois found amiss. At times, she told Harold to beat them. Unwilling to challenge his wife yet lacking her sadism, he took the children downstairs and pretended to beat them, having them yell as if they were actually in pain.

After three years of this abuse, the two older Howton children ran away. They told their stores of the hair-pulling, slapping and other punishments they received, which launched another juvenile hearing—and brought Carol Felix into the case. Reading through the previously sealed files on Dennis Jurgens, she came to the conclusion that the five-year-old had been murdered. Her efforts to have his case reopened, however, went nowhere. Years later, she told a reporter, "No one wanted to deal with this. We're talking about people who just looked the other way."[4]

Studying the Battered Child

Carol Felix and other investigators who followed her in examining the Dennis case had an advantage over the experts of 1965: Much more was known about child abuse by the 1970s, thanks to the work of a medical team led by C. Henry Kempe. Their 1962 study, "The Battered Child-Syndrome," was published in the *Journal of the American Medical Association*. The article described the Jurgens situation almost to a "T," saying the term reflected "a clinical condition in young children who have received serious physical abuse, generally from a parent or foster parent . . . It is a significant cause of childhood disability and death. Unfortunately, it is frequently not recognized . . ."[5] In 1969, Kempe gave a talk discussing his work, and one of the attendees was Archie Gingold, the judge who had presided over the juvenile court hearing to decide the custody of Robert Jurgens after Dennis's death. The details of that death dominated the hearing, and after, Gingold said, "I know that boy was killed. I just can't do anything about it."[6]

Although the Jurgenses denied abusing the Howtons, the judge in the case decided the four children should be removed from the home. Robert Jurgens had already left; at 15, he sought legal protection and ended up in a foster home. After struggling with drug abuse for several years, he straightened out and eventually became a police officer in Crookston.

For the next few years, the Jurgenses lived in obscurity, though someone had remembered the questionable circumstances around Dennis's death in 1965—and they wanted others to remember them too. Inside the record book at St. Mary's Cemetery, where the boy had been buried, was a newspaper clipping dated April 12, 1965. By the time Jerry Sherwood saw it, the clipping was yellowed with age. Jerry, a mother of four from Minnesota, read how Dennis Jurgens died of peritonitis. But the clipping went on, "The body also bore multiple injuries and bruises."[7] Those few words were enough to convince Sherwood that something awful had happened to Dennis—the young boy she had given up for adoption almost 20 years before.

TURNING THE WHEELS OF JUSTICE

Sherwood knew the name of the family who had adopted Dennis, and in 1981 she tracked down Lois Jurgens. Their phone call seemed pleasant enough: Jurgens told Dennis's birth mother that the boy had been a good, happy child. Sherwood asked for a picture of Dennis, and Jurgens promised to send one along. Six weeks passed, and Sherwood grew impatient. She called the Jurgens household again and couldn't get through. An operator informed her the number had been changed, and there was no new number listed.

For a few years, Sherwood let the matter rest. But at a friend's urging in 1986, she finally approached the White Bear Lake police department, after her children helped her track down more information about Dennis. When the chief of investigations began reading from the old file, Sherwood turned pale and began to shake. What she was hearing was the description of a young boy who had been badly abused. Dr. Michael McGee, the Ramsey County medical examiner, was called in. He came to a quick conclusion: "I looked at the autopsy protocol and said, 'It's child abuse.'"[8] The long-ago classification on the coroner's report of "deferred" was changed to homicide. That news, in October 1986, led the media to contact Lois Jurgens. The change to homicide puzzled her, she said. "This seems really farfetched to me."[9] she told the *St. Paul Pioneer Press and Dispatch*. When asked how Dennis had died, Lois said she would need to talk to a lawyer before she responded.

Thanks to Sherwood's doggedness and the dramatically different attitudes about child abuse since the early 1960s, law officials took action. In January 1987, Lois Jurgens was indicted on one count of second-degree murder and two counts of third-degree murder. Harold Jurgens was not charged.

Jurgens's trial began in May. Beforehand, she went through several psychiatric evaluations. At one point she described the love she had for children, and how badly she had wanted her own. And she said she had been depressed around the time of Dennis's death. But, she added, "I didn't do anything crazy."[10]

TRIAL AND VERDICT

Lois Jurgens entered the Ramsey County Courthouse on May 11 dressed in black. Her lead defense attorney, Doug Thomson, knew he faced a difficult path to acquit his client. He had seen the autopsy photos, showing the battered body of the dead Dennis Jurgens.

The murder was front-page news

And a new autopsy by Dr. McGee of the boy's exhumed body led him to rule the cause of death as blunt trauma, which triggered the peritonitis that killed Dennis. Thomson's only hope was to discredit the string of witnesses now ready to testify about Jurgens's abusive behavior some 21 years before.

In court, McGee expanded on his findings. The blunt trauma could not have come from a fall down the stairs, as the Jurgenses had claimed. Other witnesses, including family members, gave the details of the abuse they had seen years before: tying of the boy to his crib and the toilet, the frequent bruises, his black eyes that Lois had tried to cover with sunglasses, his loss of weight.

On May 29, the jury needed less than four hours to come back with a verdict: Lois Jurgens was guilty of third-degree murder. That verdict meant the jury didn't believe Jurgens meant to kill her adopted son. Now the trial entered a second phase, as Thomson tried to show that she was mentally ill at the time of Dennis's death. Two experts said she had suffered from paranoid schizophrenia in the past. An expert for the prosecution contradicted that diagnosis, and said that even if she had been psychotic in 1965, she was well enough to know the difference between right and wrong. The jury accepted this explanation and denied the insanity plea.

Jurgens received a 25-year sentence. In 1988, the Minnesota Supreme Court denied her appeal of the verdict. Over the next few years, Jurgens twice petitioned to be released, noting that no other women had served as much time as she had for the same offense. Finally, in 1995, she was granted parole. The release angered Jerry Sherwood, who told the media, "May God strike her dead, that's what I have to say to Lois Jurgens. I prayed for eight years that she'd die in there."[11]

Another Murder?

After Lois Jurgens was released from prison, she and Harold tried to live a quiet life in Stillwater. But in 2000, both found themselves back in the public eye, as Harold's death raised suspicions. He had suffered from heart trouble for several years and entered the hospital on January 11. Two days later, he died—a day after police received a phone call suggesting that Harold may have been poisoned by his wife. When tests showed high levels of arsenic in Harold's blood, an autopsy was performed. The results showed that Harold died of heart disease, not poisoning. Sheriff Jim Frank apologized for the suspicion that was cast on Lois and the pain it caused the family, saying, "I understand it has been an unwelcome addition to their grieving process."[12]

Racial Tensions of the Times

THE CRIME: A St. Paul police officer is killed by a sniper

PERPETRATORS: Ronald Reed and Larry Clark are accused of the killing

VICTIM: James T. Sackett

SCENE OF THE CRIME: St. Paul

WHEN: May 22, 1970

Minnesota DOC

Ronald Reed's mugshot

After the riots that erupted in Watts and in the aftermath of Martin Luther King Jr.'s assassination, racial tensions remained throughout the country in 1970. On May 1, 15,000 people gathered on the green in New Haven, Connecticut, to protest the murder trial of several Black Panthers. The Black Panther Party had formed in 1966 and four years later were still espousing racial views that troubled many white Americans. Especially troubling was the Panthers' rejection of the non-violent methods of the traditional civil rights movement. The party's official name included the words "party for self defense," reflecting the Panthers' belief that black people had to defend themselves against police brutality and a white society that tried to hold blacks down. In 1970, James Sackett became a victim of those radical views.

A FALSE REPORT, THEN GUNSHOTS

Officer James Sackett had just returned to duty on May 22, having completed a leave he took after the birth of his fourth child. Sitting in a patrol car with his partner Glen Kothe, Sackett heard the call to proceed to 859 Hague Avenue, in St. Paul's Summit-University neighborhood. Rondo Avenue, to the north, had been a primarily African-American community until the Rondo neighborhood was largely demolished during the construction of I-94 during the 1960s. The area around Hague had both black and white residents, though the population as a whole consisted largely of African Americans.

The call said that a woman was in labor at the Hague address, and the squad car reached the house just after midnight. The two officers went to the front door and found it locked. Kothe then went around to the back while Sackett remained on the front porch. Inside the apartment, two teenagers were watching TV. Roger Egge, 19, heard someone trying the front door again, so he got up to investigate. As he reached the door, he heard a shot, then saw Sackett fall to the ground. Egge told the *St. Paul Pioneer Press*, "I went out the porch door and saw him on his back or side, hollering for help. Blood was gushing out . . . the voice, it was kind of weak."[1]

The sound of the shot brought Kothe running to the front of the house, where he found Sackett bleeding from a single bullet wound to the chest. He raced for his radio and frantically called in, "There is an ambush . . . my partner is shot."[2] More police soon reached the scene, but they couldn't save Sackett's life, and they found no trace of whoever had shot him.

The emergency call to 859 Hague had been a fake. The officers had been set up so they could be easy targets for a sniper. St. Paul police were determined to find the killer, but they had almost no clues to go on. They did interview two young black men of the neighborhood, Ronald Reed and Larry Clark, who had ties to a local group that emulated the Black Panthers. Reed hoped to start a chapter in the city, after several incidents of police brutality against blacks during the previous two years. But the questioning and other investigations turned up no hard evidence against them.

Two years later, though, police did arrest Connie Trimble and charge her with murder. She had been Reed's girlfriend back in 1970, and she admitted placing the call that lured Sackett to the fatal spot. But she refused to say who told her to make the call, and Trimble was acquitted on the murder charge. She did serve some time, however, for refusing to disclose the identity of the person who directed her to make the call on May 22.

A COLD CASE REOPENED

Although Trimble's acquittal pushed Sackett's murder out of the public eye, St. Paul police didn't forget about the killing of one of their own. And as the decades passed, people in the community who had at first been reluctant to tell police what they knew about the murder became more cooperative. One was John Griffin, who said Reed confessed to him that he took part in killing Sackett. More importantly, by 2004 Connie Trimble was now ready to tell all—though for a price. Suffering from stomach cancer, the accomplice wanted several thousand dollars to tell what she knew. That included saying that Reed had told her to make the fake emergency call to set up the two cops.

Reed went on trial in February 2006. The prosecution did not argue that Reed fired the gun, though it claimed to have some evidence he was the actual shooter. Instead, the prosecution wanted to show that Reed played a major role in planning and executing the sniper attack.

One key witness was Joseph Garrett. Like Reed, he had been interested in bringing the Black Panther Party to St. Paul. Garrett said that Reed had asked him if he wanted to be part of something big and "bring down the first pig" in the city.[3] Reed's lawyer noted that Garrett himself may have taken part in the shooting. He was a former military sharpshooter and before the shooting he had warned a police officer to be wary when out on the streets.

Connie Trimble testified on February 23. She admitted that Reed had told her to place the emergency call, which she did from a pay phone. When the call was over, she and Reed went to Clark's house, just down the street from where the police would soon be arriving. But Trimble said that Reed had not planned the murder, and even suggested that she and Reed had been set up by someone else; they had been told the police would be crashing a pot party at the Hague Avenue home. Her conscience, she said, had led her to tell her story now: "God knows I regret every day what happened."[4]

Minnesota DOC

Ronald Reed

John Griffin took the stand the next day, recounting his tale of how Reed told him how powerful he had felt when he killed Sackett. But years later, Griffin said, Reed admitted he regretted the murder. Defense attorney John Pecchia questioned the credibility of both Trimble and Griffin: Trimble for taking money to testify, and Griffin, a convicted drug dealer, for looking for a reduction in the prison term he was serving.

CONVICTION AND APPEALS

The jury found Reed guilty of first-degree murder and conspiracy to commit first-degree murder. Several months later, Larry Clark was found guilty of first-degree premeditated murder while aiding another. Both men appealed their guilty verdicts. In 2008, Clark won a new trial, when the state Supreme Court ruled the judge had improperly instructed the jury. The next year, the state dropped first-degree murder charges and Clark pled guilty to conspiracy to commit murder. He was given another year of prison and then released under supervision. Reed's appeals, however, went nowhere, and he is still serving a life sentence.

ANOTHER NOTABLE MINNESOTA CRIME

PRISONERS GONE WILD

Stillwater has been the site of a prison since Minnesota's territorial days, with different buildings providing cells for the state's convicted. The state penitentiary that opened in 1914 has seen its share of notorious inmates, and it has also been the scene of crimes, when prisoners rioted for one reason or another. The largest riot came in 1953, when prisoners protested conditions there and rules they disliked. The riot led to major damage in two cellblocks, and for punishment the rioters were locked in their cells and denied food for two days. Violence is still an issue there; a 2010 gang fight involving about 70 inmates required guards to use tear gas to restore order.

Paying a High Price

THE CRIME: The largest ransom ever paid in the United States at that time leads to the release of a kidnapped wife

PERPETRATORS: Kidnappers Don Larson and Kenneth Callahan

VICTIM: Virginia Piper

SCENE OF THE CRIME: Orono

WHEN: July 27, 1972

Jay Cooke State Park; Virginia Piper was found nearby

Minnesota saw several sensational kidnappings during the twentieth century, with large ransoms paid several times. The largest ever led to the freedom of Virginia Piper, wife of Harry Piper, a former principal in the Piper, Jaffray & Hopwood investing firm. The kidnappers seem to have spent or stashed—or invested—their money wisely, as only $4,000 of the ransom was ever recovered, and the men responsible for the crime were never brought to justice.

THE KIDNAPPING, THEN FREEDOM

Then as now, Orono was an affluent community, the perfect target for kidnappers looking for an easy score. It was just around 1 p.m. on July 27, 1972, when two men wearing nylon-stocking masks stormed into the Piper home. They tied up the family's two housekeepers, found 49-year-old Virginia Piper in the garden, handcuffed her and put a pillowcase over her head, then left a note before driving her off. The note informed Harry Piper that they would be in touch with specific ransom demands. Given the remote location of the home, the kidnappers were able to make an easy escape, though the FBI noted that they were looking for two cars and men described as "heavy set and tough looking."[1] About 100 federal agents took part in the search for Piper that followed.

Soon word came of what the kidnappers wanted: $1 million in $20 bills. Through the media, Mr. Piper indicated his willingness to go along with the kidnappers' demands. Meanwhile, the two men took Virginia to a wooded area near Jay Cooke State Park in Duluth. They kept her handcuffed and left her out there during intermittent rains, feeding her bread, cheese and soft drinks. Virginia, though, ignored the food, thinking she might have to ration it. At times, she heard her two captors talk about a third man, but she never saw him. Other times, just one kidnapper was with her, and though he still wore his stocking mask, Virginia got a partial glimpse of his face. On Friday evening, when she was left alone and chained to a tree, Virginia dug at the dirt around the tree with her bare hands, hoping she could uproot it and escape. The futile effort left her with broken fingernails, though she did manage to expose the tree's roots.

By Friday night, Piper had the ransom money ready to deliver at a spot the kidnappers chose. He was given elaborate instructions to bring the money himself and ended up putting the ransom in a green Monte Carlo that he left at a Minneapolis bar. The next morning, an anonymous tip told the FBI where Virginia could be found. The federal agents had taken over the case when they became convinced the kidnappers had crossed state lines at some point in their flight. About 25 agents flew to Minnesota, then drove to Duluth and began searching the designated area, calling her name. Virginia heard the agents and responded, which helped them pinpoint her location. They found her chained to the tree, wet and crying, but basically healthy.

Speaking to the media after her release, Virginia acknowledged the huge ransom her husband paid, saying, "I felt like a very expensive parcel." She didn't feel in danger, she said, until the men left her alone on Friday night. "Then I thought, 'I'm chained to a tree here and they'll find me in November.'"[2]

THE HUNT FOR THE KIDNAPPERS

At the time of Virginia Piper's release, the FBI offered no comment about whether they had any leads as to the kidnappers' identities, but as one agent said, "We're not without hope."[3] Still, it took five years for the authorities to arrest two suspects, Donald Larson and Kenneth Callahan, on the basis of a partial fingerprint and a hair sample. The arrest and subsequent trial came just before the statute of limitations was about to run out on the crime.

At the time of their arrest, Callahan and Larson were former partners in a custom cabinet making business—former, because Larson was already behind bars. In 1976, he had murdered five people in a jealous rampage fueled by his wife's relationship with a neighbor. After a failed suicide attempt, Larson went on trial for the killings, though he did not testify. He received a life sentence for the crimes.

For the Piper kidnappings, the federal government relied mostly on circumstantial evidence. Still, it was enough to win a conviction. But when Larson and Callahan appealed the verdict, largely on the grounds that a witness who could have helped their defense was not allowed to testify, they won. The 8th U.S. Circuit Court of Appeals ordered a new trial.

Virginia Piper

THE SECOND TRIAL

The witness who could possibly set Callahan free and acquit Larson of the kidnapping was Lynda Lee Billstrom. During questioning by the FBI in 1974, she said she had heard her common-law husband, Robert Billstrom, and several other men discuss a possible kidnapping. Some of the details Billstrom gave the FBI matched some of the things Virginia Piper saw and heard during her captivity in the woods. (By this time, Robert Billstrom was dead, killed by police in 1973.)

At the second trial, Billstrom gave the testimony she was prevented from giving in 1977. Other evidence weakened the government's case, including the revelation that a fingerprint offered as evidence against the two defendants may have been altered, and discrepancies in the testimony FBI agents gave about the prints. The jury this time found Callahan and Larson not guilty, even though for the first time, Virginia Piper testified that she recognized Callahan's profile, after failing to do so in previous police line-ups or in court. That claim wasn't enough to earn the government a guilty verdict. As one juror said after, "We just figured there was a lack of evidence. Very much so a lack of evidence."[4]

For Callahan, the verdict meant he could go back to cabinet making at his home in Wisconsin. For Larson, though, the verdict just meant a return to Stillwater State Prison to finish his life sentence. And for the FBI, the final verdict meant a major kidnapping case would go unsolved.

ANOTHER NOTABLE MINNESOTA CRIME

A DEADLY HATE CRIME

Spring of 1979 was not a good time to be a gay man strolling through Loring Park in Minneapolis. A string of beatings targeting homosexuals started there that May and culminated with the brutal attack on Terry Knudsen. On June 6, Knudsen was walking through the park when three men jumped him. Using a metal pipe, they beat him until he was unconscious. The attack left Knudsen with one eye missing and severe brain injuries. He died a little over a week later. His murderers were never found, and Knudsen died the same day another Twin Cites man was the victim of a hate-crime killing. Knudsen is still remembered today by gay-rights activists who are trying to stop violence against the GLBT community.

A FUGITIVE FOUND

For several years during the 1970s, the exploits of the Symbionese Liberation Army filled the news. Their most famous activity was kidnapping heiress Patty Hearst, then having her take part in some of their crimes, including several bank robberies. Kathleen Soliah had been friends with an early member of the SLA, and when its leaders came to her in 1974 for help, she obliged. She gave them some money and later took part in another robbery, during which a bystander was shot and killed. As police closed in on the gang and arrested them, Soliah fled to Minnesota. There, she adopted the name Sara Jane Olson and began a life as a loving wife and mother. She learned to cook. She acted in local theaters. She kept current on world affairs. People in Highland Park who knew Sara were amazed to learn about her previous life as Kathleen. The news came as Sara Jane Olson was arrested as a fugitive in 1999. Two years later, she pled guilty to trying to blow up police cars decades before. Olson/Soliah spent seven years in a California prison then returned to the life she had created for herself in Minnesota.

The SLA's logo

A Murder in the Family

THE CRIME: An heiress is killed in her mansion, and her adopted daughter is a prime suspect

PERPETRATORS: Confessed killer Roger Caldwell; and Congdon's adopted daughter and Caldwell's wife, Marjorie

VICTIMS: Elisabeth Congdon and Velma Pietila

SCENE OF THE CRIME: Duluth

WHEN: June 27, 1977

A mugshot of Marjorie Caldwell

Chester Congdon earned a fortune from investing in Iron Range mining and lumber and used it to build a palatial estate in a wooded corner of Duluth. Called Glensheen, the house took almost four years to build and was completed in 1908. Sitting on 22 acres along the shore of Lake Superior, the home had 39 rooms with a total area of 27,000 square feet. Congdon and his wife Clara raised their two youngest children there, and their older children brought their grandchildren there for family celebrations. Glensheen was a private retreat with all the modern conveniences of the day. Clara, writing in her diary, noted, "I will have quiet neighbors."[1] She was referring to the cemetery that sat not too far away from the house. Decades later, Glensheen's aura as a symbol of great wealth would be marred, as the house would become the scene of two brutal murders.

INTRUDER IN THE HOUSE

Of the two Congdon children who spent the most time growing up at Glensheen, Elisabeth was the oldest. The sixth of the family's seven kids, she attended Vassar College and then lived the life of the multi-million-dollar heiress she was, donating money to various charities and the arts, and splitting her time between Glensheen and two other homes.

Although Elisabeth never married, during the 1930s she adopted two daughters, Marjorie and Jennifer, and raised them at Glensheen. The girls were spoiled and overly protected; when Marjorie was first allowed to walk to school, a limousine with a security detail trailed behind. As young women, Marjorie and Jennifer married and provided their mother with a number of grandchildren. As she aged, Elisabeth lived mostly alone in the sprawling home, though she did have around-the-clock assistance after suffering a stroke in 1969. The stroke left her paralyzed on one side and confined to a wheelchair. A nurse named Velma Pietila was with Elisabeth the night of June 26, 1977. A month before, she had actually retired as a member of the medical team that looked after the elderly woman. Pietila, though, had agreed to come that night to fill in, since the usual night nurses weren't available. Her husband had asked her not to go, but Pietila insisted, arriving in her almost-new Ford Granada. That Sunday night would be the last Pietila ever spent at Glensheen.

As Sunday night became Monday morning, someone was hiding in the cemetery that Clara Congdon had once written about. Roger Caldwell was a long way from his Colorado home, but he was familiar with Glensheen and its wealthy inhabitant, having visited there about a month before. He had come to see his new mother-in-law, the woman who had once set up a trust for his wife, Marjorie. But now the flow of money had been turned off, the debts were rising, and Roger thought that he knew the perfect way to boost his family's finances—kill the old woman.

Fortifying himself with booze, Caldwell broke a window so he could open the door and get inside. Walking up the stairs to his mother-in-law's room, he suddenly heard a door open in the hallway above him, then he saw a flashlight's beam cut through the dark. Velma Pietila must have heard him, and now she was coming to investigate. Caldwell was not about to let her derail his plan. After a brief tussle on the stairs, he tossed the woman aside. She ended up on a landing, moaning. Caldwell then went back down the stairs and found a suitable weapon—a brass candleholder. Even as the intruder swung at her head and arms, Pietila tried to fight him off, but it was no use. He was bigger and stronger. Caldwell left her dead on the landing and continued his ascent, the woman's blood all over him.

Finally, he reached his ultimate destination, the bedroom of Elisabeth Congdon. He had hoped to find Elisabeth asleep, but the noise of the assault on the nurse had awakened her. "Who's there?" she called.[2] Caldwell didn't reply. Instead, he carried out his plan to kill Congdon, suffocating her with a pillow. Like Pietila, she put up a fight—as much as a semi-paralyzed 83-year-old woman could. It took four minutes for Caldwell to drain the life out of her. Then, he went about the room stealing jewelry, so police would think the killings sprung from a burglary gone wrong. Later, Caldwell even claimed that was all he wanted, just some baubles to sell to pay off his and Marjorie's debts. But no one believed it—not when Marjorie stood to inherit several million dollars when Elisabeth died.

Movie Murder Mystery

Elisabeth Congdon opened up her home for many charitable activities, and she also let Hollywood use her estate as a film set. Apparently filmmakers thought Glensheen had just the right spooky charm for their 1972 mystery, *You'll Like My Mother*, starring Patty Duke and Richard Thomas. The picture tells the story of a pregnant widow visiting her mother-in-law's home for the first time. The family members include a mentally deranged son and a relative out to get the family's riches. The real-life murders that took place at the home five years later seem to keep generating some interest in the movie.

CATCHING A CROOK

Caldwell made his getaway in the nurse's Granada. Police found it at the Minneapolis-St. Paul airport. Although Duluth police told the public they thought the murders were an unintended consequence of the burglary, they already had a lead on a person with a motive to kill Congdon—the seriously indebted Marjorie Caldwell and her husband. When she and Roger came to Minnesota for the funeral, the police gathered clues, including a wicker basket

The Congdon Mansion

Caldwell had taken from the house, filled with jewelry. They found a receipt for a bag that Caldwell bought in Minnesota the morning of the murders. The police also learned that Marjorie had tried to provide an alibi for Roger when someone called looking for him at a laundromat back in Golden, Colorado, the morning after the killing. She told the caller that he had just stepped out for a drink. But laundromat employees said Roger hadn't been there at all that day.

In July, Caldwell was arrested in Bloomington, before he and Marjorie left town after the funeral. Soon he was indicted on two counts of first-degree murder. Court maneuverings, including having the case moved to Brainerd, in Crow Wing County, delayed the start of the trial until April 1978.

The prosecution relied on strong circumstantial evidence to make its case. There was certainly a motive, and there was evidence to place Caldwell in the state at the time of the murder. There were also the stolen goods found in his possession. The defense tried to suggest that other Congdon relatives who disliked Marjorie were trying to frame her husband. But Joe Kimball, the *Minneapolis Tribune* reporter who covered the case extensively, couldn't see the logic of that, since one of the Congdon relatives would had to have killed Elisabeth just to tarnish Marjorie, which seemed farfetched.

After two months, the jury reached its verdict: guilty on both counts. Caldwell received two life sentences, to be served consecutively. The prosecution, though, was not satisfied, as it figured Marjorie Caldwell had instigated the murder plot. She was charged with conspiracy to commit murder. Arrested in Duluth, she went to Hastings for the trial that would determine if she would join her husband behind bars.

TWISTS AND TURNS

Marjorie's defense was even more vigorous than her husband's. Her legal team gathered evidence that showed sloppy police work during the investigation at Glensheen. The defense was also able to cast a shadow on the character of William Furman, a private investigator some Congdon relatives had hired after the murder. Under oath, he pleaded the Fifth Amendment dozens of times as the defense questioned his work habits. The defense also suggested that Furman had tried to frame Caldwell after the fact. Finally, a waitress from Golden, Colorado, who had not testified at Roger's trial said that she saw him the evening of the murder in Golden. Without access to a private jet, it would have been hard for him to be in both Colorado and Minnesota on the same night.

During the trial, some witnesses also attested to Marjorie's good character and love for her mother. For her part, Marjorie tried to engage in small talk with the lead prosecutor, John DeSanto. When she baked a cake for her own attorney, Marjorie offered some to DeSanto too. He said, "No way I am having anything that's baked by Marjorie." In a reference few would pick up—but DeSanto did—she replied, "John, there's no marmalade in it."[3] Several years before, Elisabeth had gotten very ill after a visit from Marjorie. She recovered, but Elisabeth's nurses speculated that Marjorie might have poisoned her mother's marmalade sandwiches. The marmalade story didn't emerge until after the 1977 murders.

Marjorie's legal team had more luck, or skill, than Roger's, and she was acquitted. She had won over several of the jurors, who offered her hugs when the trial was over. That verdict prompted Roger to seek a new trial, since evidence that helped his wife's case could possibly prove his innocence too. In 1982, the Minnesota Supreme Court agreed, and Caldwell won a second trial. Free as he waited for it, Caldwell headed to his hometown of Latrobe, Pennsylvania.

As a 1983 trial date neared, Duluth officials decided they didn't want to go through another trial, especially one they could lose. Attorneys on both sides worked out a deal: Caldwell would plead guilty to two charges of second-degree murder, and the time he had already served would be his sentence. Caldwell returned to Latrobe but struggled to find work as he battled his past and alcohol abuse. He finally killed himself in 1988, but not before leaving a note in which he recanted an earlier confession.

MARJORIE'S LIFE OF CRIME

For the "innocent" Marjorie Caldwell, her associa-tion with her mother's murder turned out to be the least of her legal worries. During her trial, Marjorie spent time with an old family friend, Wally Hagen, who came with his wife Helen to attend some of the proceedings. When Helen ended up in a nursing

Marjorie Caldwell

home with Alzheimer's, Marjorie began seeing Wally. She made a trip to visit Helen too, bringing food that she fed the stricken woman. Somewhat mysteriously, Helen died a few days later, and people who knew about the marmalade sandwich suspicions raised their eyebrows again. But since that matter was still not public, no toxicology report was done. Marjorie soon married Wally, spent time in North Dakota (where she was charged with, but never prosecuted for, bigamy), and then headed to Arizona. To her stepson Tom Hagen, Marjorie was a loose cannon. "She just goes off. And when she goes off, she's totally out of control. I mean it's like a maniac."[4]

In the years to come, Marjorie would "go off" several times. She served time in Minnesota for arson and an even longer stint in Arizona for an arson that was part of a planned insurance fraud. In 2008, she was convicted again, this time for forgery. She was charged with killing Wally Hagen too, but was released for lack of evidence. In 2010, an Arizona court refused her plea to reduce the terms of her probation so she could enter a nursing home.

Back in Duluth, Glensheen is now a museum owned by the University of Minnesota. For many years, tour guides did not mention the killings that brought the home to national attention. Now, though, they are a little more open about the events of June 27, 1977.

Bring in the DNA

Roger Caldwell's "I did it—I didn't do it" statements about the Congdon murders may have raised some doubts about his role in the crime. But in 2003, DNA evidence seemed to show that he was at the scene of the crime. Prosecutor John DeSanto had kept an envelope that had been introduced as evidence. It contained a coin stolen from Glensheen that had been mailed from Duluth to Colorado on June 27. Saliva on the sealed envelope was traced with 99.93 percent certainty to Roger Caldwell.

Obsession Turns Violent

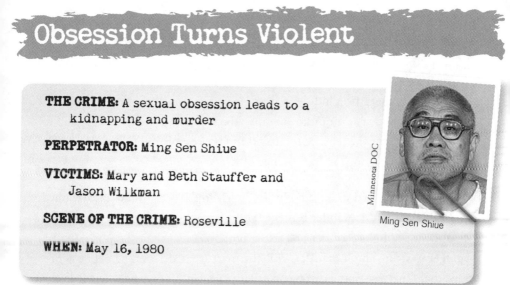

THE CRIME: A sexual obsession leads to a kidnapping and murder

PERPETRATOR: Ming Sen Shiue

VICTIMS: Mary and Beth Stauffer and Jason Wilkman

SCENE OF THE CRIME: Roseville

WHEN: May 16, 1980

Minnesota DOC

Ming Sen Shiue

During more than 150 years of statehood, Minnesota murders have come in all types: murders for money or to knock off gang rivals, murders that sprung from moments of anger, killings of innocent bystanders during burglaries gone wrong. But no murder case had all the twisted elements of the one that began during the 1970s and reached its culmination in 1980. Amid a kidnapping, repeated rapes, and a courtroom knife attack, the murder that occurred during Ming Sen Shiue's spree of mayhem almost seems incidental—though certainly not to the parents of the six-year-old boy who just happened to be in the wrong place at the wrong time.

FROM CLASSROOM OBSESSION TO CRIME

In 1965, Mary Stauffer was a math teacher in Roseville. One of her students was Ming Sen Shiue, a Taiwanese immigrant. His family had settled in Roseville after his father took a job at the University of Minnesota. Ming's father died when the boy was about 11, and Ming took it upon himself to be the man of the house. In his mind, that meant punishing his younger brothers—sometimes severely. He used a belt in one instance; in another, he stuck one of his brothers in the oven, which he then turned on. Ming's behavior also included some inappropriate sexual feelings toward his mother. At one point, he surreptitiously cut a hole in her nightgown, hoping to see her exposed vagina.

Outside the home, Ming indulged in some petty crimes that landed him in juvenile court and sent him into therapy. The frustrated therapist assigned to the case wrote that the teen lied, refused to take responsibility for his actions, and seemed "like a dog" in his absence of true emotions.[1]

Mary Stauffer seemed to have no inkling of Ming's background as he took her algebra class at Alexander Ramsey High School. Stauffer caught the eye of her student, though, who was just seven years younger than she was. He soon began fantasizing about Stauffer while he masturbated. Then he began writing sexual fantasies. Some involved sexual violence; if not rape, then at least intercourse that caused the woman pain. And often, Mary Stauffer was the victim of Ming's deviant fantasies. He found he derived pleasure by thinking about causing her pain.

While indulging in these fantasies about his former math teacher, Ming seemed to have created a persona that impressed others. He played varsity football and his classmates voted him Most Likely to Succeed, and he left Ramsey and headed off to college. But after two years he dropped out—in part because of his growing obsession with Mary Stauffer.

FROM FANTASY TO REALITY

By 1975, writing about his perversion with Stauffer wasn't satisfying enough; he decided to make his violent fantasies a reality. He hatched a plan to kidnap Stauffer, thinking he had located her house in Duluth. But when the time came to carry out the crime, Shiue soon realized he had made a mistake. The house he targeted belonged to Stauffer's in-laws. Confronting them with a gun, he tied them up and threatened to come back and kill them if they reported the home invasion to the police.

Still wanting to find his fantasy lover, Ming continued to search for her. He didn't know that the Stauffers were in the Philippines, serving as missionaries.

But when they came back to Minnesota for a year before planning to head to Asia again, Shiue was able to track down where Mary Stauffer and her family lived. He began stalking her, and even made several attempts to break into her home. Finally, on May 16, 1980, he approached Mary and her 8-year-old daughter Beth as they walked out of a hair salon.

Mary noticed the Taiwanese man and thought perhaps he was lost and wanted to ask directions. Instead, he pulled a gun out of his pocket, put it close to Beth's body, and said, "I need a ride."[2] He forced the mother and daughter into their car, with Mary behind the wheel and Beth in the front seat with Shiue's gun at her head. After a while, in a wooded area of Anoka County, Shiue had Mary stop the car, then he forced the two victims into the trunk, where he tied them together and gagged them.

As Shiue drove, he twice stopped the car to check on his prey. During the second stop, a small boy approached the car after Shiue had opened the trunk. Before Jason Wilkman could get out more than a few words, he found himself locked inside the trunk with the Stauffers. Soon he began to cry.

Shiue took off again, then stopped at the Carlos Avery Wildlife Refuge, near the town of Forest Lake. Shiue opened the trunk and pulled out Jason. He also grabbed a metal bar. When he returned to the car, he was alone; Jason's bludgeoned body was left under some birch trees near the edge of a cornfield.

Shiue's home, the scene of the crime

Finally, Shiue reached his final destination, his home in Roseville, where he had already prepared a space to hold his captives, a closet empty except for some bedding and a bucket to use as a toilet. Both captives were blindfolded. Shiue startled Mary when he called her by her first name; she had not used it in his presence. "You know me," she said. "How do you know me? Who are you? I want to know—who are you and what do you want?"[3] Mary would learn everything the next day.

SEVEN WEEKS OF TRAUMA

After feeding his captives breakfast, Shiue took Mary out of the closet. Then with a video camera rolling, he explained their past relationship to her. He spun a tale of the woe that had befallen him since his days at Ramsey High—a fate he laid at Mary's feet. She had undeservedly given him a bad grade, which kept him from going to college and avoiding the draft while the Vietnam War raged. Sent to fight overseas, he had been captured and sent to a prison camp. Once he was freed, he said, he came home and couldn't find a good job. All because of Mary. And all completely untrue. Then he raped Mary Stauffer, while the camera continued to record the assault. Shiue would tape more of his rapes in the weeks to come.

The closet where the Stauffers were held

For a time, Shiue kept the Stauffers in the closet. Eventually he let them come out, mother and daughter chained together, and watched carefully as Mary prepared meals for them. Once he even drove them to Chicago, when he had to go there for a work-related event. He made careful preparation in a rented RV so he could keep them confined and silent. On July 4, he took them out to see fireworks. As on the Chicago trip, his threat of killing them and anyone they might seek out for help keep the Stauffers in line.

But on that excursion, Mary saw a Ramsey County sheriff's car, with a phone number printed on the side. Mary memorized the number. And in a few days, she would have the chance to use it. The distorted version of domestic life that Shiue had created with his captives made him complacent. On July 7, he went to his electronics-repair business and did not barricade the closet door. Inside, Mary managed to remove the hinge pins from the door and leave the closet, Beth tied to her side. They went to the phone and dialed the number she had seen on the police car a few days before. The two victims went outside and hid behind a tree as they waited for help to come.

THE TRIAL

A little later, with the Stauffers safely rescued, police arrested Shiue at his business. The same day, the Wilkman family learned the news about their missing son. In a quirk of fate, the handcuffed Shiue crossed paths with the Stauffers at the federal court building. Shiue called to Mary, "Why did you run?"[4]

Plans to Kill

While in jail, Shiue offered to pay another prisoner, Richard Green, $50,000 if he would kill the Stauffers and help him escape. Green instead passed the information along to the FBI, though the court did not find the claim credible. Shiue also fashioned a crude weapon out of a broken light bulb and toilet plunger, part of a plan to carry out his own escape. Whether Shiue wanted the Stauffers dead before they could testify is unknown, but years later he did admit he had murder on his mind when the two were his captives. He said he would have killed them while he still had control of them, if they had not escaped first.

Shiue faced two trials: one in federal court for kidnapping, and one in state court for the murder of Jason Wilkman. For the federal trial, the defense based its case on proving Shiue was insane at the time of the crimes. Three medical experts testified to his psychotic state, with one saying Shiue was "so blinded by his obsession . . . (that) he did not consider (his behavior) to be immoral because it was predestined."[5] On the stand, Shiue did not deny his crimes but played up the insanity angle, testifying that he sometimes had auditory and visual hallucinations (a claim that years later he admitted was a lie). The prosecution's expert witnesses, however, said someone as supposedly delusional and psychotic as Shiue could not have been so astute in carrying out his crime, evading police, and even running his business.

During the trial, as Mary Stauffer approached the stand to testify, Shiue rose from his chair and lunged at her. Federal marshals quickly sprung into action and grabbed him. But during the second trial, the security was not so tight. As Mrs. Stauffer again went to testify, this time about her experience with Jason Wilkman, Shiue charged at her, wielding a knife he had snuck into the courthouse. Trial judge Robert Bakke described what happened next: "[Shiue] . . . raced hollering toward Mrs. Stauffer on the witness stand. He jumped on her, tipped over the witness chair, came down on top of the witness."[6]

Reporters captured snippets of the dialogue as the scene unfolded, with court officials yelling "Get him, get him," and Stauffer pleading, "Oh, my God! Someone do something."[7] It took five men to get Shiue off of Stauffer, but not before he sliced her face, leaving a gash that required 62 stitches.

The attack stunned the courtroom, and led to a hearing to determine if Shiue was competent to contribute to his defense. The answer was affirmative, the trial continued, and he was convicted of second-degree murder; prosecutors had reduced the charge from first-degree murder after Shiue agreed to show them where he had dumped the boy's body. For the Wilkman murder, Shiue received 30 years. The sentence in the federal case was life, with the two sentences to be served concurrently.

Shiue was not always a model prisoner: In 1982, prison officials heard reports that he was planning on shanking another prisoner. Years later, he did assault another prisoner, and as court records indicate, he "acted aggressively towards the correctional officer who intervened."[8] Some of the violence may have been in self-defense, since convicts who committed sexual crimes or mistreated children are often targeted for abuse by fellow prisoners, and that was Shiue's experience.

FREEDOM?

By the summer of 2010, Ming Sen Shiue was eligible for parole. Before his hearing, Minnesota law officials wanted to make sure that if Shiue ever got out of prison he would not be free to live as he pleased in the state. Anoka

County prosecutors petitioned to have him civilly committed as a sexually dangerous person and a sexually psychopathic personality. The district court had to decide if Shiue still presented a danger to society, given the nature of his crimes and his psychological makeup. If Shiue were civilly committed, he would undergo evaluation and then face another hearing to see if he should remain committed. At the time, more than 500 people had entered the program, and none had been released.

By 2010, Shiue was 59 and suffering from arthritis and tremors. His attorney said Shiue posed no risk, if he did win parole. The district court, though, said Shiue met the legal criteria for being civilly committed as a sexually dangerous person, and the Court of Appeals upheld that decision in 2011. At that time, Shiue had still not been granted parole. But if he were, he would have to enter the Minnesota Sex Offender Program. As two of the medical experts who testified in 2010 said, Shiue still had not really come to terms with the nature of his acts or sought help for his sexual deviancy. In 2014, after a legal challenge by Shiue, the Court of Appeals upheld that Shiue could be civilly committed indefinitely if he ever won freedom from federal prison.

Mother and Victim Meet

The 2010 commitment hearing for Ming Sen Shiue brought a flurry of media attention to the details of his 30-year-old crimes. The media also interviewed his surviving victims, particularly Mary Stauffer, with ABC News doing a major story on her ordeal. After Shiue's convictions, Mary and her husband resumed their missionary work and tried to lead as normal a life as possible. Beth grew up, married, and raised a family. Both Mary and Beth attended the commitment hearing. So did Mei Dickerman—Shiue's mother. She and Mary Stauffer talked for 20 minutes and their conversation ended with hugs and a prayer. Stauffer said, "As a mother, if I had a son who did what Ming did, I would feel so horrible. I let her know how much I feel for her. My suffering ended in seven weeks, but it lasts for the Shiue family forever."[9]

Murder on the Farm

THE CRIME: Two bankers are murdered on an abandoned farm

PERPETRATORS: Steve and James Jenkins

VICTIMS: Rudy Blythe and Toby Thulin

SCENE OF THE CRIME: Lincoln County

WHEN: September 29, 1983

Minnesota DOC

Steven Todd Jenkins

Farmers are used to the cycles of boom and bust that make their lives so challenging. Weather and changes in supply and demand play a part, and so do rising prices for equipment and supplies. For some farmers, being in debt year to year adds to their stress. In 1983, farmers in rural Minnesota were facing one of those difficult times; for some, it was the worst farming crisis since the bleak days of the Great Depression. And as in that historic downturn, farmers weren't the only ones hurting. Abandoned family farms and other larger economic forces at work made life hard for small-town lenders such as Rudy Blythe, owner of the Buffalo Ridge State Bank in Ruthton.

TRYING TO FARM

Blythe had come to Minnesota from the East to fulfill his dream of buying a small-town bank and using its resources to help local citizens. And he tried to help James Jenkins realize his dream, but perhaps no one could have helped the farmer, a Lincoln County native. Jenkins had approached Blythe for a $30,000 loan in 1979 to help operate his dairy farm. Blythe gave him the loan, even though Jenkins had a history of bad credit.

Jenkins had struggled for most of his adult life, trying to earn enough to support his family. His parents had struggled too, on their small farm, but through hard work they succeeded and eventually sold their land for a profit. Growing up, James worked on the farm, but his real interest, neighbors recalled, was machines. One said, "He could fix machinery like no one in the area."[1]

As an adult, James went back and forth between farming and operating, renting and fixing machines. But neither avenue led to much financial security for him and his family—wife Darlene and children Steven and Michele. He went through foreclosure in 1967. Seven years later, he bought a farm that he later sold for a profit, but he had racked up a string of debts along the way.

Jenkins tried again to farm in 1977, buying his small dairy operation a few miles outside Ruthton. Banker Blythe might not have seen the paperwork at Buffalo Ridge State Bank that showed some of the Jenkinses' earlier financial hardships. He gave Jenkins the loan he wanted, and the farmer used it to fix up the house and buy farm animals.

Life, though, did not really improve for the family. The farm was too small to run an efficient dairy operation, and James and Darlene were facing marital problems. By 1980, she wanted a divorce, weary of the constant stream of financial troubles and attracted to a new beau.

The divorce led Jenkins to default on his loan with Buffalo Ridge and declare bankruptcy. Until that time, though, he had always made his payments to the bank. The divorce, not a larger farm crisis, led to the loss of the family home. But whatever the cause, all Rudy Blythe knew was that his bank owned a farm that would prove hard to sell.

ROAD TO THE CONFRONTATION

With the personal and financial loss, James Jenkins drifted for a time and finally ended up in Texas. He did all right there, working odd jobs and saving cash. By the fall of 1982, he had saved enough to buy a trailer. He sent for Steven to come live with him, and the teen helped his father do maintenance work for a school district. Steven was notable for the military garb he liked to wear, and he sought out veterans to discuss weapons. From his father's boss, Charles Snow, he learned how to shoot an M-1 semi-automatic rifle.

When he returned to Minnesota in 1983, Steven spent time practicing with the gun and even took it with him into his bedroom at night. His self-imposed training regimen included running some distance and then stopping to shoot, a technique he picked up from Snow. Along with training like a commando, Steven wore a soldier's close-cropped haircut, and tattoos covered his arms. One was of a pair of battle axes. Another was of Sylvester the cat.

Life in Texas

To the people of Brownwood Texas, James Jenkins seemed like a nice, hardworking man. Learning he was a suspect in a double murder threw off many of the people who knew him. He had come to Brownwood penniless, but his skill at fixing machinery got him a job with the local school district. For a time, he slept in a shed, until he earned enough money to buy a trailer. James Lancaster, the district superintendent, liked Jenkins, but he wasn't so sure about his son. He couldn't put his finger on it, but he described Steven in the words his own son would use: "Kind of one brick shy of a load."[2]

Steven Jenkins had left Texas for Minnesota in February, and his father followed him that summer. James was once again ready to try his hand at dairy farming, but he found it hard to get a loan. He began to suspect—correctly—that the burned Rudy Blythe was telling other bankers that Jenkins was a credit risk.

On September 28, after another refusal from another bank, Jenkins snapped. Using a fake name, he called Blythe to schedule an appointment at his old farm. "Ron Anderson" told Blythe he was interested in buying the old Jenkins place. To his son, Jenkins said, "We are going to go there and rob and scare him, scare the hell out of him."[3]

The next day, father and son loaded up their pickup with a small arsenal: two shotguns, a handgun and an M-1, along with several defused grenades, knives, and other military equipment, all of it Steven's. They arrived at the farm about 90 minutes before the appointed time. They were startled a little later when Blythe, along with Toby Thulin, a loan officer at the bank, pulled up in a green station wagon. Each Jenkins grabbed a gun and then ran to hide.

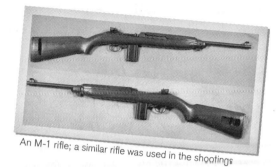

An M-1 rifle; a similar rifle was used in the shootings

As a rain fell, Blythe and Thulin saw a white pickup with Texas plates outside the farmhouse. Blythe and Thulin began to investigate the property. As they did, another car drove in, and behind the wheel was Blythe's wife, Susan. She had come out to the farm to switch cars with her husband. Instead, Blythe instructed her to go get the sheriff, since trespassers were obviously somewhere on the property. And given the Texas plates, he suspected James Jenkins could be involved.

As Susan left, Blythe and Thulin returned to their car. Then, the shots began. The first one hit the windshield of the station wagon. The next one passed through the passenger-side window vent and entered Thulin's neck. The bullet severed his spinal cord, and his lifeless body fell out the open car door. The third shot wounded Blythe in the back. The injury, though, was not bad enough to keep the banker from scrambling away from the car and heading toward the nearest neighbor, about a half mile away. But as he ran, the next round of shots began. The shooter had moved when Blythe did and was only about 90 feet away as he fired four times, hitting Blythe with each one. He fell into a ditch and died soon after.

With both of their victims dead, the murderers ran for their truck and took off. They drove for a few hours before making a stop—to buy more ammo for the M-1. Back on the road, they spotted a Rock County sheriff's car tailing them. James turned his pickup down a gravel road and told Steven to get out and shoot at the officer. He fired off three rounds. The deputy sheriff at the wheel ducked down and sped away. The Jenkinses then began their escape, taking a route that would bring them back to Texas. Meanwhile, police identified them as the suspects in the double murder at their old home, and a nationwide manhunt began. And while the national media talked about revenge as a possible motive for murder, some farmers who protested against bank foreclosures saw the killings as an aberration from their nonviolent methods. In the words of Eric DeRycke, a farm protest leader in Minnesota, James Jenkins was a "screwball." He added, "We have no sympathy for Jimmy Jenkins."[4]

TEXAS TROUBLES, MINNESOTA TRIAL

On Saturday, October 1, the Jenkinses rolled into Paducah, Texas. The next day, with the two men broke and hungry, Steven went to the local police department to turn himself in, leaving his father behind at the abandoned farm where they'd taken refuge. He told police about the crimes that had taken place in Minnesota, and about his father hiding out on the farm. Steven said the older man had been talking about suicide. He led the police to their hideout. When they arrived, they saw James Jenkins' body lying along the side of the dirt road. Looking closer, they saw that not much was left of his head, as he had shot himself with a shotgun. Steven said his father had been alive when he left.

Back in custody in Minnesota, Steven gave his version of what had happened at his family's old farm. Yes, he had supplied weapons and gone along with his father to rob and scare the bankers. But Steven denied taking part in the killings. He claimed not even to have seen the shooting; he just heard gunfire and shouts. His father was the murderer. His story did not sway a grand jury, given the evidence—though circumstantial—that the state presented. In late October, Steven was charged with murdering Rudy Blythe and Toby Thulin.

IN COURT

The granite courthouse in tiny Ivanhoe, county seat of Lincoln, hummed with activity as Steven Jenkins went on trial in April 1984. His was the first murder trial the county had seen in more than 80 years. The prosecution focused on several facts to try to convince the jury that the teen was a killer. For one, he owned all the weapons found in the truck, including the murder weapon, the M-1. Steven Jenkins was also known to have trained extensively with the gun and proven himself a good shot. His father had no reputation as a marksman. And the young, strapping Steven could have easily run after the fleeing Blythe that September morning on the farm. His father was overweight and suffered from retinitis pigmentosa, an eye disease that was slowly robbing him of his sight. He lacked the agility and the ability to carry out the two murders.

Defending Jenkins was perhaps the most colorful defense attorney in the county, Swen Anderson. A large man with a booming voice and penchant for swearing, he would grow close to Steven and eventually adopt him. During the trial, Anderson wanted to suggest that Steven had endured the barbs of an emotionally unstable and abusive father. The son would do anything the father asked—like going to the farm to intimidate, or even kill, Rudy Blythe. But Anderson asserted, as Steven did, that James Jenkins was the killer. Anderson hoped to play up a medical report that talked about Steven's non-violent nature, ignoring testimony that described his more violent side. And the attorney hoped to introduce evidence from the father's past that showed his explosive tendencies and menacing threats. But Anderson's efforts were thwarted as the prosecution successfully argued for excluding the expert testimony and other evidence Anderson hoped to introduce. The defense attorney basically had no case to present, and the state was not willing to plea bargain.

The trial took less than three weeks, and the jury then took ten hours to find Steven Jenkins guilty of the first-degree murder of Blythe and second-degree murder of Thulin. For the more serious charge, he was sentenced to life in prison. The case was appealed to the state Supreme Court, which upheld the verdict.

Oak Park Heights State Prison

YEARS LATER

Jenkins was sent to Oak Park Heights State Prison to serve his sentence. He would be eligible for parole in 2001. Several months before then, Jenkins stunned some Minnesotans who had been involved in the case. On an A & E Network documentary, a tearful Steven Jenkins Anderson admitted that he had killed the two men in 1983. Michael Cable, one of the prosecutors at the trial, said, "I was as surprised as anyone else when he admitted it."[5] He added that the public show of remorse might have been calculated to win sympathy for Anderson at his parole hearing. But the hearing came and went with Anderson remaining behind bars. Several more followed, and each time Anderson's request for parole was denied. Finally, though, in 2013, Tom Fabel, the lead prosecutor in the Jenkins trial, helped begin the process to win Anderson his freedom. He was released in 2015.

One Crime, Two Views

As the Jenkins case unfolded, a popular spin on it was that it reflected the frustration of farmers grappling with a financial crisis. Andrew H. Malcolm covered the case for *The New York Times* and largely took that attitude. He turned his reporting on the Blythe-Thulin murders into a book that developed the same theme, *Final Harvest: An American Tragedy.* When the book came out in 1986, Malcolm called the story "a wonderful allegory for the troubled Midwest. It had troubled farmers and troubled bankers."[6] And farmers' advocates believed that the desperation of the time could have led a farmer to snap. But Minnesota historian Joe Amato had a different interpretation: "You had a peculiar murder by a father and son who were a peculiar father and son."[7] Amato pointed out that James Jenkins failed as a farmer even when others in Minnesota were succeeding. He wrote *When Father and Son Conspire* (1988) to refute Malcolm's thesis and develop his own. The Jenkinses, he argues, had "an agreement . . . to destroy themselves."[8]

ANOTHER NOTABLE MINNESOTA CRIME

DAVID BROM TOOK AN AXE . . .

Minnesota DOC

David Brom

By many accounts, David Brom was a troubled teen in 1988, when he used an axe to butcher his parents, sister, and brother. Police recorded more than 50 blows on the bodies, and the murders rocked the Broms' well-to-do community of Cascade Township. Brom was an A-student at the Catholic high school he attended in Rochester, but friends reported he had recently argued with his father, and as his trial showed, he suffered from mental illness. Even the prosecutor conceded that, yet under Minnesota law, Brom was not disturbed enough to be found not guilty by reason of insanity.

A 2011 report in the *Star Tribune* noted that Brom had basically grown up behind bars, and had been mostly a model prisoner. But given his four life sentences, three to be served consecutively, he will not be up for parole until 2041.

A Mystery Resolved

THE CRIME: An eleven-year-old boy is abducted

VICTIM: Jacob Wetterling

PERPETRATOR: Danny Heinrich

SCENE OF THE CRIME: St. Joseph

WHEN: October 22, 1989

FBI

The sketch of the suspect

A parent's worst nightmare came painfully true for Patty and Jerry Wetterling. Attending a party on a Sunday night, they got a call that changed their family's life forever. Their 11-year-old son, Jacob, had been abducted at gunpoint. The kidnapping set off a massive manhunt and pledges of donations to pay for a possible ransom. But the police search proved futile, and no ransom note ever came. Instead, the people of St. Joseph became wary, keeping a more watchful eye on their kids. And the Wetterlings took steps to try to help other children who might be in danger, even when the passage of time suggested that Jacob wouldn't return.

OUT FOR A VIDEO

Jacob Wetterling, his younger brother Trevor, and a friend named Aaron Larson were home on a Sunday evening, along with the Wetterlings' youngest child, Carmen. Patty and Jerry Wetterling trusted the boys alone with Carmen, and left them with a pizza before heading off to a friend's house. At the party, Patty received a call from home: the boys wanted to rent a video at a local convenience store. Patty later said that her first internal reaction was, "No, it's starting to get dark."[1] When the phone was passed to Jerry, he heard a barrage of arguments that convinced him to let the boys go to the store. A neighbor's daughter came over to watch Carmen as the three boys headed off.

On the way back from the store, about a half mile from the Wetterlings' house, a man wearing a mask stepped out of the shadows by the end of a driveway. In his hand was a gun. He told the boys to lie face down in a ditch by the side of the road. He asked them their ages. Hearing Trevor was 10, the gunman told him to get up and run away, or he'd shoot. Aaron said he was 11. The man had him roll over, then told him to run as well. Finally, he grabbed Jacob.

Aaron and Trevor obeyed the masked man, though after running about 100 yards Trevor looked back. Jacob and the man were gone. Footprints in the gravel at the end of the driveway suggested that at some point Jacob began to resist his captor, but with little result. At the Wetterling house, Trevor told the babysitter to call 911. Instead, she called her father, who called the police. When the Wetterlings got the call about the abduction, they left the party without saying a word and headed home. Talking to the police, seeing the terror on the children's faces, Patty couldn't believe what was happening. She later said, "I had always thought you were more at risk in the Twin Cities. That's where real crime happens . . . not in St. Joseph."[2]

The local fire department joined in the search for the missing boy, while a state police helicopter with a searchlight hovered overhead. The FBI was soon called in, and by the morning media across the state were reporting on the abduction. As days passed with no sign of Jacob, the national press reported on the story as well.

LOOKING FOR CLUES

The statistics on kidnapping at the time showed that it was rare for a child to be abducted by a stranger. Looking at the facts of the Wetterling case, the FBI decided that Jacob had probably been taken by a sexual predator. They called in a local expert on such cases, a retired Hennepin County detective named Ned Neddermeyer. One angle he began to investigate was that the abductor might work around children, as a bus driver perhaps, or a teacher. Neddermeyer and the officers worked feverishly at the beginning, putting in 16-hour days every day, then cutting back to 12 to reduce burnout. Early on, they got several dozen leads, but none of them amounted to anything concrete.

Meanwhile, as weeks passed, and then months, the Wetterlings wrestled with their conflicting feelings. "I don't lose hope," Patty said six months after the kidnapping. "But I haven't lost touch with reality either"—the reality that "maybe he's not coming home."[3]

By the end of 1989, with nothing concrete to work with, the FBI pulled several agents off the case, then another half-dozen. In the spring, helicopters did an aerial search of quarries in the St. Cloud area but found nothing, other than a number of false leads incorrectly linking Wetterling neighbor Dan Rassier to the crime.

As the investigation scaled back, Jacob's parents didn't give up. In fact, their untiring activism led to some major changes in the U.S. legal system. One was the passage of the 1994 Jacob Wetterling Act. Patty walked the halls of Congress with former representative Jim Ramstad to win backing for the bill. It called on each state to create registries of convicted sex offenders and a national sex offender database. The Wetterlings also helped found a non-profit foundation now called the Jacob Wetterling Resource Center, which is dedicated to keeping all children free from abuse, exploitation, or abduction.

THE MYSTERY, SOLVED

In the years that followed those developments, new technology helped police pursue a lead against a new suspect. Starting in 2014, the investigators did a cold-case review of the Wetterling murder and a serious of unsolved sexual assaults that took place in Minnesota during the late 1980s. Clothing found at the scene of one of the assaults contained DNA evidence. That evidence led the FBI to Danny Heinrich of Annandale, Minnesota. Police had actually questioned him in 1989 and 1990 about both the Wetterling disappearance and the kidnapping and assault of another young boy from the region, but Heinrich was never charged. Thanks to the DNA evidence that linked Heinrich to that other kidnapping, investigators searched Heinrich's house, where they found child pornography. Heinrich soon became a person of interest in the Wetterling case. In 2016, Heinrich made a deal with the authorities. He confessed to killing Wetterling. In return, government lawyers said they would not prosecute him for that murder, though he still faced 20 years for

TITLE XVII—CRIMES AGAINST CHILDREN

Subtitle A—Jacob Wetterling Crimes Against Children and Sexually Violent Offender Registration Act

SEC. 170101. ESTABLISHMENT OF PROGRAM.

(a) IN GENERAL.—

(1) STATE GUIDELINES.—The Attorney General shall establish guidelines for State programs that require—

(A) a person who is convicted of a criminal offense against a victim who is a minor or who is convicted of a sexually violent offense to register a current address with a designated State law enforcement agency for the time period specified in subparagraph (A) of subsection (b)(6); and

(B) a person who is a sexually violent predator to register a current address with a designated State law enforcement agency unless such requirement is terminated under subparagraph (B) of subsection (b)(6).

(2) COURT DETERMINATION.—A determination that a person is a sexually violent predator and a determination that a person is no longer a sexually violent predator shall be made by

The Jacob Wetterling Act

receiving child pornography

As part of the plea agreement, Heinrich led police to the spot near Paynesville where he had buried Wetterling almost 30 years earlier. In court, with the Wetterling family in attendance, he described how he had abducted, molested, and then killed Jacob on that long-ago October night. Heinrich said, "I am truly sorry for my evil acts."[7]

After his name was cleared, Dan Rassier, wrongly accused for so many years, sued a former Stearns county sheriff and investigators who once linked him to the crime.

The Angry Heir

THE CRIME: Animosity during a divorce leads to murder

PERPETRATOR: Russell Lund Jr.

VICTIMS: Barbara Lund and her boyfriend E. Kevin Kelly

SCENE OF THE CRIME: Minnetonka

WHEN: August 5, 1992

Star Tribune

Russell Lund Jr.

For many Minnesota residents, the name Lunds symbolizes a quality shopping experience. Russell Lund began marketing upscale food products before World War II, then ended a relationship with a Twin Cities partner, which led him to open grocery stores bearing his name. By the mid-1980s, the Lunds stores were generating sales of about $100 million each year, and the Lund family had real estate and oil holdings to augment their wealth. But while most people associated the Lund name with good food, in 1992 it became linked with a domestic spat turned bloody.

LIFE AS JUNIOR

When Russell Lund Sr. stepped down as company head in 1973, he turned the reins over to his nephew, not Russell Jr., though the son sat on the board of directors. When other changes came at the top in 1991, it was founder Lund's grandson, Russell III (also called Tres), who took over. Each time, Russell Jr. was passed over, and with the latter move he was forced off the board as well. But the second-generation Lund didn't seem to mind not being involved with the family business, which he found boring—perhaps especially after serving as a military pilot during the Korean War. He had his hobbies, including operating ham radios and collecting guns. For the most part he lived simply, though he did build a nice home on a hilltop in Minnetonka, to take advantage of better reception for his radios. He also liked to fly, and he and his second wife Barbara shared a passion for planes.

Despite the millions Lund owned thanks to his family's success, he couldn't avoid personal mishaps and tragedy. In 1974, he crashed a twin-engine Cessna, though no one on board was seriously injured. The same year, his 14-month-old daughter Christiana died in a drowning accident. That loss seemed to unsettle him, and over the next several years he was arrested twice for shoplifting. The second arrest led to Lund's undergoing a psychological evaluation, which came back with a diagnosis of kleptomania.

Through the '80s, Lund struggled with a business venture of his own. In 1968, he and several other pilots started Flight Training Center, which later morphed into Flight Transportation Corp., a charter-flight company based at Flying Cloud Airport in Minneapolis. Shady business dealing by his partners led the company and Lund into several court battles, and neither Lund nor the company fared well. As recently as 1992, Lund was still in court trying to recover more than $800,000 he had lost due to his partners' illegal activities. And amidst that, he was still dealing with a divorce that his wife Barbara had initiated in 1989. The unsettled split had turned ugly as the two argued over Barbara's share of his estimated $11 million in assets.

LAST NEGOTIATIONS

Barbara Lund, according to those who knew her well, was a lively, energetic and attractive woman—qualities that years before had earned her the title of Miss Minneapolis. Barbara was also a woman who didn't back away from a challenge. Despite her husband's wealth, she built a career for herself as a real estate agent. And as the divorce proceedings with Russell dragged on, her lawyers became aggressive as well, preparing to seek information from the Lunds Company via subpoena. They wanted to see how his father's company and Russell were linked financially; Russell disliked this prying into the family affairs.

He was probably also not thrilled to see that Barbara was often with her new boyfriend, E. Kevin Kelly. A lawyer and former state lawmaker in Iowa, Kelly later became a lobbyist. Whatever Lund's feelings for Kelly, by the summer of 1992 the tense relation between the two spouses had ratcheted up another level. Barbara was sure that her estranged husband was tapping her phone. She also believed that Lund had entered their Orono home to search for papers relating to the divorce. She usually stayed in Orono when she was in Minnesota. Most of the time, though, she tried to avoid the state as the divorce progressed.

As July ended, Russell Lund faced new legal pressures. Barbara's attorney had filed a contempt of court motion for Russell's failure to pay certain money he owed Barbara. Russell worried about the hearing and what would happen if he went to jail. But both sides were still on speaking terms, and the Lunds, along with Kelly, met in Orono to try to reach an understanding. The talks seemed to go well, but money was still a sticking point. Russell made what he said was a final offer of $4 million, which didn't seem to satisfy Barbara. Still, she and Kelly were ready to meet with him one more time, at the Minnetonka home, before her attorneys served the Lunds Company with a subpoena.

A "CRIME OF THE CENTURY"

On August 6, Minnetonka police chief Richard Setter received a phone call from Minneapolis lawyer David Roston. The attorney said he wanted to meet with Setter to tell him about the "crime of the century" that had just occurred in Minnetonka. At around 6:45 p.m., Setter met Roston and a private investigator at a local hotel. Then, at 7:00, well-known defense attorney Joe Friedberg arrived. From drug dealers to judges, people in trouble eagerly sought his services. And now Russell Lund had as well. Friedberg and Roston began to explain why they had called Setter: two dead bodies were lying inside Lund's Minnetonka home. Russell Lund had killed them the night before.

After Russell had committed the murders, he had called his divorce attorney, who then called in David Roston. That set in motion a chain of events that some later questioned as unethical. The whole day of August 6, Roston and Friedberg were busy. They hired a private investigator who gave police the gun used in the murder. They also arranged for Lund to check into a psychiatric hospital under an assumed name. They did all this before they contacted Chief Setter, later maintaining that they were required to do all this to protect their client.

The crime shocked the Twin Cities

Hearing Roston's shocking news, Setter sent several of his officers to look inside the Lund home. Seeing nothing from outside, the police obtained a search warrant and broke down a locked door to enter the home. There was no sign of forced entry, and when news of the murder became public, Setter assured worried neighbors that this was not a random act of violence: "The incident appears to be isolated and specifically directed at the two victims."[1]

The two victims were found in different parts of the house. Barbara's body was at the foot of the stairs in the basement, shot three times. Kelly was hit four times, including twice in the head. His body was on the first floor. The police found a trail of blood through the house, and evidence that the killer had tried to clean up after himself.

"Celebrity" Lawyer

Successfully defending a wide range of crooks can earn a lawyer a degree of fame, and Joe Friedberg had achieved that even before joining Russell Lund's legal team. Not flashy like some well-known defense attorneys, Friedberg was known in Minnesota for his modest demeanor in the courtroom, backed by a willingness to take risks and delve into human nature. His successes before 1992 include winning the acquittal of a man alleged to have committed murder with a shotgun and then to have driven around with the dead body in his truck for several days. He also argued the first successful insanity defense in the state in decades. In 2009, Friedberg took on a different kind of case, when he helped out old friend Norm Coleman in his recount battle with eventual U.S. Senator Al Franken.

LEGAL PROCEDURES

It was Friedberg who, on August 8, finally told police where Lund was and arranged for the police to talk to him. The lawyer said Lund would come in to be fingerprinted if he weren't arrested, and district attorney Dan Mabley agreed. Lund showed up wearing blood-stained shoes, which the police took as evidence. He then returned to the psychiatric hospital.

On the 19th, Lund was arrested but not charged and freed on $400,000 bail. He then spent some time at a Connecticut psychiatric institution before coming back to Minnesota. At the end of the month, he was charged with two counts of first-degree murder, and his bail mushroomed to $10 million. Dan Mabley explained the lag in bringing formal charges by saying his people "wanted to make sure they'd done the most thorough investigation possible. We are confident all the facts we have now are accurate."[2]

County attorneys cited Lund's wealth when calling for the increased bail, which they wanted to be set at $15 million. Friedberg argued that the original bail was high enough. He called the new amount "an overreaction; it's overcompensation because Mr. Lund happens to come from a wealthy family."[3] Of course, outside the courtroom some people felt Lund had already received preferential treatment because of that wealth. And Friedberg was able to get his client released from jail and sent for psychiatric treatment, delaying an arraignment until November. As one county attorney later admitted, "It was pretty clear that he was a very sick man and he needed medical help."[4]

While Lund waited for his trial, the case continued to make news. The *Star Tribune* sought to have the Lunds' sealed divorce file released. When Minnesota courts agreed, Lund's attorney asked U.S. Supreme Court Justice Harry Blackmun to keep them secret, arguing that releasing them would violate Lund's privacy and harm his right to a fair trail. Blackmun refused to intercede. Meanwhile, bits of the prosecution's case emerged, as a search warrant affidavit showed that Lund had been at his home the morning of the 6th, with the two dead bodies. The prosecution learned from the company that handled Lund's home security system that he had answered a call that morning about a false alarm.

THE END

Back at the Fairview Riverside Medical Center, where he had earlier spent time, Lund underwent his psychiatric treatment. He was held in a locked ward under almost constant surveillance. On October 31, a staff member checked in and found that Lund was fine. But sometime during the next 15 minutes, Lund executed a plan he'd been thinking about for weeks. Taking out a plastic bag he had secretly stashed on his body, he put it over his head. When the staff made its next check at 7:15, they found the man suffocating. He was pronounced dead less than an hour later.

Lund's suicide shocked his attorneys and left the brother of victim E. Kevin Kelly feeling somewhat cheated. "It's a way to wrap it up," John Kelly said, ". . . but it may have been more satisfying to have a trial and have him sentenced."[5] The suicide also did nothing to stop rumors about Lund's activities, fed by some of the documents in his criminal file. Bruce Rubenstein outlined some of them in his 2006 book *Greed, Rage, and Love Gone Wrong: Murder in Minnesota*. According to Rubenstein, an informant told the FBI that Lund had gone to chief Richard Setter after the murder, confessed and showed him the murder weapon. The informant claimed that Setter let Lund leave and did not take the gun. If true, Rubenstein explains the chief's actions as the reaction of a friend rather than a law enforcement official, as he and Lund had been pals, sharing an enthusiasm for guns.

Rubenstein also mentions that right before the murder, Lund gave a local TV station documents relating to the legal troubles of FTC. With the murders, the station dropped any investigation it may have planned, and the documents were never released.

Those rumors and speculations remain just that today. The only thing definitive about this crime? It led to the deaths of three people and was fueled by money and perhaps a touch of madness.

The Death Pact

When Russell Lund first thought about suicide, he shared his thoughts with Zachary Persitz. A Russian immigrant charged with killing and dismembering a friend, Persitz met the millionaire while they were both in the Hennepin County Jail, before Lund's return trip to Fairview Medical Center. Persitz said the two men were drawn to each other because they were both intellectuals. During their conversations, they discussed possible methods of killing themselves—including covering their heads with plastic bags, as Lund later did. Persitz attempted it too, shortly after Lund's suicide. But unlike his friend, the Russian was noticed by the guards before he lost consciousness. "I did it like we planned," Persitz said ". . . only he succeeded."[6] Persitz was later sentenced to life for murder, and 18 years later he tried again to kill himself while behind bars. This time it worked. In June 2010, Stillwater State Prison officials found Persitz hanging in his cell.

A Cold Case of Murder

The parking lot where the body was found

THE CRIME: A woman's body is found in the trunk of her car after she is brutally murdered

PERPETRATOR: Unknown

VICTIM: Anne Barber Dunlap

SCENE OF THE CRIME: Minneapolis

WHEN: January 1, 1996

Murder can happen any time, any place—even on a trip to the mall. Anne Barber Dunlap set out to buy shoes on December 30 at the Mall of America. She never returned home. A frantic husband and concerned parents waited for news about the missing 31-year-old, only to have their worst fears confirmed when she was finally found two days later, murdered. As in many killings, police focused first on who might have a motive, and they fixed their attention on Dunlap's husband, Brad. Anne had just recently increased her life insurance policy to $1 million. But she and Brad seemed like the perfect couple: happily married, successful in their jobs, building a new home, hoping to start a family. Dunlap repeatedly claimed his innocence while the police searched fruitlessly for clues about the killing.

A NORMAL WEEKEND, AT FIRST

During the holidays of December 1995, Brad and Anne were living with Anne's parents on the south end of Lake Calhoun, while builders worked on their new Medina home. Brad had no trouble living temporarily with his in-laws, and the two couples got along as if they were best friends. The Dunlaps spent many weekends at the Barbers' cabin in Annandale, and they even vacationed together. During the two months Anne and her husband lived with the Barbers, her parents saw even more clearly the love they shared. And they saw how well Brad treated Anne, his kindness and generosity, paired with an even temperament that led him to seek compromise rather than disagree with his wife.

On December 30, a Saturday, Anne set out with her running group for a ten-mile jog. After brunch with her friends, she came home around 2:00 p.m. and told Brad she was going shoe shopping at the mall. Brad had his own errands to run, so they made plans to rendezvous later that afternoon and then go out to dinner. The Barbers were out at their cabin. When 6:00 p.m. rolled around, Anne had not returned from the mall. As time passed, Brad grew concerned, since his wife was always punctual and responsible. He finally called the Barbers around 8:00 p.m. to tell them he hadn't heard from Anne. The Barbers drove home from the cabin, following a route Brad thought Anne might have taken. Her parents stopped in different parking lots, hoping to see Anne's red Toyota Celica, but they didn't find it. As they searched, Brad made phone calls to the Mall of America, to hospitals, to the police. No one had any information on his wife.

The next morning, Brad called the Minneapolis police to report Anne's disappearance. Friends and family went out to more area shopping centers, hoping to spot her car in a lot. Brad spoke to a reporter for the *Star Tribune* and said, "This is so uncharacteristic of her. I just know something has gone wrong."[1]

On New Year's morning 1996, the Dunlaps' friends continued their search for Anne's car. In the parking lot of the K-Mart at North Lake Street and Nicollet Avenue, one group saw the Toyota, but no sign of Anne. They called Brad and notified police. The officers told them to stay away from the car, which still had its keys inside. The police

The parking lot where Anne's body was found

towed the car to the forensics garage, where they opened the trunk. Inside they found blood all over, and Anne's dead body. Her throat was slit, and stab wounds covered her head and neck. Her diamond ring had also been taken.

THE INVESTIGATION

Within several hours of their discovery, the police called in Brad Dunlap for questioning. After five hours of grilling, he went to the Barbers' home, crying, telling them about Anne's death, and that the police said he was a suspect. He told his in-laws he had nothing to do with the murder. They believed him and Dunlap remained in their home as the investigation went on.

The police came to the house on the night of January 1 and again on the 4th, looking for clues. As attention focused on Brad, rumors began to spread. One said the Barbers had refused to give police blood samples; not true, the couple later told the media. And while the police did take samples from bloodstains they found in the house, Louise and Donn had explanations for the source of the stains—their own recent household accidents.

Perhaps most damning to Brad was the report that Anne had just recently increased her life insurance police to $1 million. Her parents confirmed that, but said the change came at the suggestion of a financial planner Anne had contacted. Given the couple's new home and plans to start a family, both she and Brad thought it made sense to increase coverage for both of them.

The picture of Brad and Anne's "storybook romance" also took a blow. Brad's former business partner said the couple had gone through several years of marital counseling. And to the police, bloodstains found in the Barbers' garage were suspicious, though they did not conclusively link them to the killing. After several weeks, the police admitted they had no hard clues to link Brad to the murder, though he remained their prime suspect. After his initial cooperation on the 1st, he grew less cooperative, while maintaining his innocence. His lawyer Paul Engh said, "I think he's been maligned by something he did not do."[2] Several weeks later, a lawyer for the Barbers said that Brad's activities on December 30, as much as they could be independently confirmed, were those of "someone who doesn't know his wife is dead."[3]

LEGAL BATTLE

While police never charged Brad Dunlap with his wife's murder, he remained the chief suspect, and public opinion throughout 1996 remained against him. Friends reported that strangers spat on him while he jogged, and he endured many stares and whispers that were directed his way. By the summer of 1997 he had had enough of the unwanted attention. Brad quit his job and moved to Arizona.

Although not charged for the murder, Brad still found himself tangled in a legal battle. Chubb, the company that carried Anne's life insurance, refused to pay the claim, saying that he had been planning to kill his wife even before she took out her new policy. Brad sued Chubb, saying the company and the Minneapolis police were working together to thwart his receiving the payment.

Anne Barber Dunlap

Several court dates were postponed, and finally, in October 1998, Chubb and Dunlap settled the case out of court. Donn Barber, representing his daughter's estate, said, "We're pleased and he's pleased."[4] But details of the settlement were not released.

After that, Dunlap kept a low profile in his new home state. He did give one interview in 2005 to TV station WCCO. He said, "There really isn't a day that goes by that I don't think of Anne."[5]

His former in-laws continued to believe in his innocence and they remained close to him after his move to Arizona. As of 2016, the Barbers were hopeful that new leads or DNA evidence would help police track down their daughter's killer.

While true-crime fans might have their own personal favorites, some are bound to be left out or given short shrift in a book of limited scope. Here's a handful of other notable crimes committed in Minnesota; it's just enough information to pique your curiosity and perhaps entice you to learn more about them.

A SERIAL KILLER STRIKES

By the time Andrew Cunanan was found dead from a self-inflicted gunshot wound in July 1997, he had made national news as the murderer of fashion designer Gianni Versace. But that was just the last in a string of murders that started in a Minneapolis apartment several months earlier. Cunanan was bright, charming and gay. He also had a large chip on his shoulder from failed romances and money problems. And by early 1997 he had taken an HIV test.

Cunanan's wanted poster

Though he never got the results, he probably thought he was positive. In the midst of all that, he had become convinced that two men he had earlier wooed had begun an affair together while both were living in Minneapolis. In April he came to the city to visit them. In a rage, he killed one of them, Jeffrey Trail. The other man, David Madson, was stunned, but he helped Cunanan wrap up the body in a rug. Then the killer and his accomplice let the dead body sit in Madson's apartment for several days. When they learned that someone in the building had found out about Trail's body, they left the city. Outside Minneapolis, Cunanan shot Madson, then began his killing spree that would end with Versace's death in Miami's trendy South Beach.

THE 20TH TERRORIST

Zacarias Moussaoui

Flight instructor Clancy Prevost grew a little suspicious when he heard one of the new students at the school had paid for most of his tuition in cash, with $100 bills. But to his bosses, money was money, so Zacarias Moussaoui began his classes at the Pan Am International Flight Academy in Minneapolis, Minnesota, where he hoped to learn to pilot a 747 airplane. Prevost, though, remained wary of Moussaoui, especially since he had such limited flight experience. Prevost kept Moussaoui from using a simulator on his own, and he alerted the FBI about the new student. Soon, federal agents were questioning Moussaoui and then placing him under arrest for immigration issues. Further digging revealed that he might have ties to a terrorist organization—and he did. It turned out that Moussaoui was the so-called twentieth hijacker who was supposed to take part in the September 11, 2001, Al-Qaeda attacks. Thanks to the sharp thinking of Prevost, Moussaoui ended up in a federal prison, rather than a martyr for Al-Qaeda.

THE MISSING SLIPPERS

Ruby slippers at the Smithsonian Institution

When a pair of red slippers went missing from a Grand Rapids museum during the summer of 2005, a few people panicked. These weren't just any red shoes—they were one of the five pairs of red slippers made for Judy Garland to wear in *The Wizard of Oz*. The shoes were worth about $1 million, so officials at the Judy Garland Museum were devastated with the theft. The shoes were loaned to the museum for several weeks by a collector of Hollywood memorabilia; an earlier loan of the slippers had gone off without event. In 2011, San Diego police executed a search warrant to explore the home of a collector there, but they didn't find the slippers. As of mid 2013, they were still unaccounted for.

STEALING BIG BUCKS

Tom Petters

To investors, Tom Petters seemed liked the epitome of success, as he bought electronic goods from wholesalers, then made money selling the merchandise to retailers. The investors wanted in on the action, which had enabled Petters to build a massive multi-million-dollar home in Wayzata, on Lake Minnetonka. While the home was real, Petters' business was no more than a house of cards—a $3.65-billion Ponzi scheme that collapsed in 2008. The fraud was one of the largest of its kind carried out in the United States, and it netted Petters a 50-year sentence in a federal penitentiary.

VENGEANCE WITH A GUN

Andrew Engeldinger

Reuven Rahamim was a perfect example of the successful immigrant entrepreneur. His Minneapolis sign business was poised for more growth in 2012, when he fell victim to an all-too-familiar scenario: a mass shooting. A disgruntled employee named Andrew Engeldinger knew he was about to be fired, so he took out a gun, shot several co-workers, his boss, and a UPS driver who happened to be at the store. Then Engeldinger turned the gun on himself. Six people in all died on September 27, making it one of the worst mass killings in state history.

CHAPTER NOTES

A Husband's Slow Death

[1] *Pioneer & Democrat*, March 16, 1859, p. 3.

[2] *Pioneer & Democrat*, March 15, 1859, p. 3.

[3] *Pioneer & Democrat*, March 16, 1859, p. 3.

[4] *Ibid.*

[5] *Ibid.*

[6] *Ibid.*

[7] Matthew Cecil, "Justice in Heaven: The Trial of Ann Bilansky," *Minnesota History*, Winter 1997–1998, p. 356.

[8] *Ibid.*, p. 361.

[9] *Ibid.*

[10] *Pioneer & Democrat*, March 24, 1860, p. 3.

[11] *Ibid.*

A Robbery Gone Wrong

[1] Cole Younger, *The Story of Cole Younger, by Himself*, available online at http://www.gutenberg.org/files/24585/24585-pdf, p. 103.

[2] *Ibid.*

[3] T. J. Stiles, *Jesse James: Last Rebel of the Civil War* (New York: Vintage Books, 2002), p. 326.

[4] *The Story of Cole Younger*, p. 108.

[5] *Jesse James: Last Rebel of the Civil War*, p. 328.

[6] *Ibid.*, p. 329.

[7] Walter N. Trenerry, *Murder in Minnesota: A Collection of True Cases* (St. Paul: Minnesota Historical Society Press, 1985), p. 91.

[8] *The Story of Cole Younger*, p. 113.

[9] *Ibid.*, p. 116.

[10] *Ibid.*, p. 117.

[11] Minnesota Historical Society, available online at http://www.mnhs.org/library/find-aids/00861/pdf/00861-000001.pdf.

[12] *The Story of Cole Younger*, p. 127.

[13] *Minneapolis Tribune*, July 11, 1901, p. 2.

The Murder of Kitty Ging

1 Edward H. Goodsell, *Harry Hayward* (Minneapolis: Calhoun Publishing Company, 1896), available online at http://books.google.com/books?id=h6A_AAAAYAA-J&printsec=frontcover&source=gbs_ge_summary_r&cad=0#v=onepage&q&f=false, p. 4.

2 *Murder in Minnesota*, pp. 145–146.

3 *Harry Hayward*, p. 103.

4 *Ibid.*, p. 108.

5 "Crazy Adry Hayward," *San Francisco Morning Call*, February 12, 1895, p. 4.

6 *Ibid.*

7 "Testified Against His Brother," *The New York Times*, February 12, 1895, n.p.

8 *Harry Hayward*, p. 91.

9 *Minneapolis Tribune*, December 11, 1895, p. 1.

10 *Ibid.*

Family Matters

1 "Who Killed Louis Arbogast?" *St. Paul Pioneer Press*, September 15, 1909, p. 1.

2 *Ibid.*, p. 5.

3 "Girl is Hysterical," *St. Paul Pioneer Press*, September 14, 1909, p. 1.

4 "Who Killed Louis Arbogast?" p. 1.

5 *Murder in Minnesota*, p. 173.

6 "Will Not Be Tried on Murder Case," *Austin Daily Herald*, October 26, 1909, p. 1.

The Wife Gets It

1 "Saw Her Ten Days Ago, Husband Tells Police," *St. Paul Pioneer Press*, April 27, 1917, p. 2.

2 "Tried to Save Sister from Killer's Bullet," *ibid.*

3 Giles Playfair, "Is the Death Penalty Necessary?" *The Atlantic*, September 1957, available online at http://www.theatlantic.com/past/docs/unbound/flashbks/death/playnec.htm.

The Circus Lynchings

1 John D. Bessler, *Legacy of Violence: Lynch Mobs and Executions in Minnesota* (Minneapolis: University of Minnesota Press, 2003), p. 184.

2 "West Duluth Girl Victim of Six Negroes," *Duluth Herald*, June 15, 1920, pp. 1, 3.

3 *Legacy of Violence*, p. 187.

4 *Ibid.*, p. 192.

5 "Three Negroes Lynched in Duluth Last Night," *St. Cloud Daily Times*, June 16, 1920, page 8.

6 *Ibid.*

7 *Legacy of Violence*, p. 212.

8 *State v. Mason* (Supreme Court of Minnesota, June 9, 1922) Northwestern Reporter 189, p. 455, available online at http://books.google.com/books?id=cw48AAAAIAAJ&pg=PA452&lpg=PA452&dq=max+mason+appeal+minnesota+circus&source=bl&ots=vUBAZPWKJi&sig=UfuuW2g6L-5TUW5KSBxMkngoHids&hl=en&sa=X&ei=XrVAUeLkGOmxyQHA7IHYD-Q&sqi=2&ved=0CFwQ6AEwBg#v=onepage&q=max%20mason%20appeal%20minnesota%20circus&f=false.

When the Criminal Becomes the Victim

1 Paul Maccabee, *John Dillinger Slept Here: A Crooks' Tour of Crime and Corruption in St. Paul, 1920–1936* (St. Paul: Minnesota State Historical Society Press, 1995), p. 12.

2 Lincoln Steffens, "The Shame Of Minneapolis: The Ruin and Redemption of a City that was Sold Out," p. 15, available online at the Minnesota Legal History Project, http://minnesotalegalhistoryproject.org/assets/Steffens-%20Shame%20of%20Mpls.pdf.

3 *John Dillinger Slept Here*, p. 5.

4 *Ibid.*, p. 65.

5 "Danny Hogan Slain; Victim of Auto Bomb," *St. Paul Dispatch*, December 5, 1928, reprinted online at http://blogs2.startribune.com/blogs/oldnews/archives/52.

6 *Ibid.*

7 *Ibid.*

8 "Bomb in Auto Kills Underworld Ruler," *The New York Times*, December 5, 1928, n.p.

A Favorite Madam

1 Meridel Le Suer, *Ripening: Selected Work* (New York: Feminist Press at CUNY, 1990). p. 41.

[2] *John Dillinger Slept Here*, p. 13.

[3] *Ibid.*, p. 15.

[4] "Early Trial is Probable," *The Evening Tribune*, December 15, 1913, p.1; "State Finishes in Graft Case," *The Evening Tribune*, February 13, 1914, p.1.

The Willmar Bank Robbery

[1] *Machine Gun Kelly*, Alcatraz History.com, http://www.alcatrazhistory.com/mgk.htm.

[2] Brad Smith, "The Verne Miller Story: From Lawman to Outlaw," *South Dakota Magazine*, available online at http://southdakotamagazine.com/the-verne-miller-story.

[3] "Willmar Bank Raiders Seize $50,000," *The Evening Tribune*, July 15, 1930, p. 1.

[4] *Ibid.*

[5] *John Dillinger Slept Here*, p. 94.

[6] *Ibid.*, p. 92.

[7] The Legend of "Machine Gun Kelley," FBI.gov, https://www.fbi.gov/news/stories/2008/september/kelly_092608.

A Famous Kidnapping with Local Ties

[1] "Lindbergh Will Pay Ransom for Baby," *The Evening Tribune*, March 2, 1932, p. 4.

Snatching Millionaires

[1] Tim Brady, "Crime Capital," *Minnesota Monthly*, http://www.minnesotamonthly.com/media/Minnesota-Monthly/April-2007/Crime-Capital/.

[2] *John Dillinger Slept Here*, p. 106.

[3] *Ibid.*, p. 143.

[4] *Ibid.*, p. 150.

[5] "Dunn's Story of Ransom," *The New York Times*, June 20, 1933. p. 9.

[6] *John Dillinger Slept Here*, p. 154.

[7] FBI Bremer Investigation Summary, p. 10, available online at http://vault.fbi.gov/barker-karpis-gang/bremer-investigation-summary/Barker-Karpis%20Gang%20Summary%20Part%201%20of%201/view.

[8] "Kidnappers Free Bremer on a Payment of $200,000; Wide Manhunt is Pushed," *The New York Times*, February 8, 1934, p. 1.

[9] FBI Bremer Investigation Summary, p. 31.

One Who Got Away

1 *People & Events: John Dillinger*, 1903–1934, from "Public Enemy Number 1," American Experience, http://www.pbs.org/wgbh/amex/dillinger/peopleevents/p_dillinger.html.

2 Elliott J. Gorn, *Dillinger's Wild Ride: The Year That Made America's Public Enemy Number* One (New York: Oxford University Press, 2009), p. 61.

3 "Dillinger Escapes from Indiana County Jail," *Evening Journal*, March 3, 1934, p. 1.

4 *John Dillinger Slept Here*, p. 219.

5 *Ibid.*, p. 221.

6 *What I Knew About John Dillinger*, from "Public Enemy Number 1," American Experience, http://www.pbs.org/wgbh/amex/dillinger/filmmore/ps_confess.html.

7 "Doctor Claims Dillinger Threatened to Kill Him," *Moorhead Daily News*, May 19, 1934, p. 1.

8 *What I Knew About John Dillinger.*

Beating the Rap—As Usual

1 "Kid Cann," St. Louis Park Historical Society, http://www.slphistory.org/history/kidcann.asp.

2 Marda Liggett Woodbury, *Stopping the Presses: The Murder of Walter W. Liggett* (Minneapolis: University of Minnesota Press, 1998), p. 66.

3 Herbert Lefkovitz, "Inquiry is Lagging in Liggett Death," *The New York Times*, December 29, 1935, E11.

4 *Stopping the Presses*, pp. 182–183.

5 "Kid Cann Acquitted in Liggett Murder," *The New York Times*, February 19, 1936, p. 1.

Robbery Leads to Murder

1 Curt Brown, "Half-century Hasn't Blurred Memories of Officer's Death," *Star Tribune*, May 10, 1999, available online at St. Paul Police Historical Society, http://www.spphs.com/history/lee_startribune_19990510.php.

2 Hi Paul, "Death Grazes Photographer as Bandit Slays Detective," *St. Paul Pioneer Press*, September 11, 1949, p. 1.

3 "Half-century Hasn't Blurred Memories of Officer's Death."

The Dentist Did It

[1] "Dentist Doped Them, Patients Tell Police," *Austin Daily Herald*, April 26, 1955, p. 1.

[2] Larry Millett, *Murder Has a Public Face: Crime and Punishment in the Speed Graphic Era* (St. Paul: Borealis Books, 2008), p. 33.

[3] "Dentist Doped Them, Patients Tell Police."

[4] *Murder Has a Public Face*, p. 51.

[5] "Witness Says Axilrod Made Very Damaging Admissions," *Fergus Falls Daily Journal*, October 19, 1955, p. 4.

[6] Richard Helgerson and Jack Page, "4 More Women Say Dentist Kept Them Drugged," *Minneapolis Tribune*, April 25, 1955, p. 1.

[7] *Murder Has a Public Face*, p. 52.

[8] Richard Helgerson and Jack Page, "Dead Woman's Sister Tells Story on Dentist," *Minneapolis Tribune*, April 26, 1955, p. 1.

[9] *Murder Has a Public Face*, p. 51.

[10] "Jury Expected to Get Axilrod Case Monday," *Winona Daily News*, October 29, 1955, p. 5.

[11] *Murder Has a Public Face*, p. 109.

[12] "Axilrod to Get Freedom After 9 Years," *Fergus Falls Daily Journal*, August 11, 1964, p. 5.

The Family That Slays Together

[1] Officer Robert H. Fossum, Minnesota Law Enforcement Memorial, http://www.mnlema.org/fallen_insert.php?officer_id=130.

[2] "Badly Wounded Killer Tells Story," *Fergus Falls Daily Journal*, September 17, 1957, p. 1.

This Gun For Hire

[1] "Slaying Details Related in Court," *The New York Times*, November 27, 1963, n.p.

[i] William Swanson, *Dial M: The Murder of Carol Thompson* (St. Paul: Borealis Press, 2006), Kindle edition, Chapter 1, Section 4.

[3] "Mastrian Enters Trial Testimony," *Fergus Falls Daily Journal*, November 14, 1963, p. 1.

[4] Barbara Davidson, "'Nub City' and Other Stories of an Insurance Investigator," *The New York Times Magazine*, March 12, 1972, p. 37.

[5] *Dial M*, Chapter 2, Section 12.

[6] "Thompson Guilty in Death of Wife," *The New York Times*, December 7, 1963, n.p.

[7] Caroline Lowe, "Cold Case: T. Eugene Thompson," WCCO, October 13, 2007, http://minnesota.cbslocal.com/2007/10/13/cold-case-t-eugene-thompson/.

One Mother's Cruelty, Another's Love

1. Dan Chu, "A Tale of Two Minnesota Mothers: One Seeks the Truth Behind Their Son's Death, the Other Stands Accused," *People*, March 2, 1987, available online at http://www.people.com/people/archive/article/0,,20095740,00.html.

2. *State of Minnesota v. Lois Germaine Jurgens*, Court of Appeals of Minnesota, April 27, 1988, available online at http://mn.findacase.com/research/wfrmDocViewer.aspx/xq/fac.19880427_0003.MN.htm/qx.

3. "A Tale of Two Minnesota Mothers."

4. Barry Siegel, "Child Murder: The Town Confronts Its Past," *Los Angeles Times*, February 29, 1988. Available online at http://articles.latimes.com/1988-02-29/news/mn-205_1_child-abuse.

5. C. Henry Kemp, et al. "The Battered-Child Syndrome," *Child Abuse & Neglect*, Vol. 9 (1985), p. 143, available online at http://www.kempe.org/download/The_Battered_Child_Syndrome_sm.pdf.

6. Barry Siegel, *A Death in White Bear Lake* (New York: Ballantine Books, 1990), p. 226.

7. "Child Murder: The Town Confronts Its Past."

8. Brian Bonner, "Boy's Death Ruled Homicide After His Case Re-examined," *St. Paul Pioneer Press and Dispatch*, October 28, 1986, p. 1A.

9. *Ibid.*, p. 14A.

10. *A Death in White Bear Lake*, p. 450.

11. "Mother Who Beat Boy to Death Goes Free," *Deseret News*, June 6, 1995, available online at http://www.deseretnews.com/article/463063/MOM-WHO-BEAT-BOY-TO-DEATH-GOES-FREE.html?pg=all.

12. "Jurgens Died of Heart Disease," *Brainerd Dispatch*, February 15, 2000, available online at http://brainerddispatch.com/stories/021500/new_0215000006.shtml.

Racial Tensions of the Times

1. Al McFarlane, "He Saw Slain Officer Collapse," *St. Paul Pioneer Press*, May 23, 1970, p. 1.

2. Shannon Prather, "Lawyers Begin Courtroom Duel Over Officer's 1970 Slaying," *St. Paul Pioneer Press*, February 22, 2006, available online at http://www.accessmylibrary.com/article-1G1-142390210/lawyers-begin-courtroom-duel.html.

3. Marisa Helms, "Trial Begins in 36-Year Old Cop Killing," Minnesota Public Radio, February 21, 2006, available online at http://minnesota.publicradio.org/display/web/2006/02/21/sacketttrial.

4. Shannon Prather, "Witness: Sackett Suspect at Scene," *St. Paul Pioneer Press*, February 23, 2006, p. 5A.

Paying A High Price

1 "Stock Official's Wife Kidnapped," *St. Paul Pioneer Press*, July 27, 1972, p. 1.

2 "Released Woman Recalls Fears When Abductors Left Her Alone," *The New York Times*, July 31, 1972, n.p.

3 Wayne Wangstad, "Agents Heard Mrs. Piper," *St. Paul Pioneer Press*, July 30, 1972, p. 2.

4 "Second Trial Acquittals," *Minneapolis Tribune*, December 7, 1979, n.p.

A Murder in the Family

1 *Glensheen: The Historic Congdon Estate*, https://glensheen.wp.d.umn.edu/explore/mansion/.

2 Joe Kimball, *Secrets of the Congdon Mansion* (White Bear Lake: Jaykay Publishing, 2009), Kindle Edition, "The Introduction," n.p.

3 Cindy Chapman, "Minnesota's Most Infamous Heiress: the Newest Chapter," KARE11, July 30, 2004, available online at http://www.kare11.com/news/news_article.aspx?storyid=59684.

4 *Ibid.*

Obsession Turns Violent

1 In the Matter of the Civil Commitment of Ming Sen Shiue, Tenth Judicial District, State of Minnesota, September 20, 2010, available online at http://www.wdio.com/kstplmages/repository/cs/files/20100929134440552.pdf.

2 Donna Hunter et al. "Mind Games: Dangerous Obsession Leads to Horrific Kidnapping," ABC News, June 21, 2010, available online at http://abcnews.go.com/Primetime/primetime-mind-games-math-teacher-kidnapping/story?id=10952017.

3 Eileen Bierant, "Mary Stauffer Stalked by Former Math Student Ming Shiue" *Citypages*, February 10, 2010, available online at http://www.citypages.com/2010-02-10/news/mary-stauffer-stalked-by-former-math-student-ming-shiue/.

4 *Ibid.*

5 *United States v. Ming Sen Shiue* (650 F2d 919), United States Eighth Circuit Court of Appeals, June 5, 1981, available online at http://openjurist.org/650/f2d/919/united-states-v-ming-sen-shiue.

6 In the Matter of the Civil Commitment of Ming Sen Shiue.

7 Wayne Wangstad, "Shiue Attacks Mrs. Stauffer," *St. Paul Pioneer Press*, February 9, 1981, available online at http://www.twincities.com/localnews/ci_14521217

8 In the Matter of the Civil Commitment of Ming Sen Shiue.

9 David Chanen, "Shiue's Mother, Victim Share a Talk, and Hugs," *Star Tribune*, April 22, 2010.

Murder on the Farm

1 Joseph Amato, *When Father and Son Conspire: A Minnesota Farm Murder* (Ames: Iowa State University Press, 1988), p. 34.

2 Wayne King, "Minnesota Farmer's Violence Shocks Texans Who Knew Him," *The New York Times*, October 5, 1983, available online at http://www.nytimes.com/1983/10/05/us/minnesota-farmer-s-violence-shocks-texans-who-knew-him.html?pagewanted=all.

3 *State of Minnesota v. Steven Todd Anderson*, Minnesota Supreme Court, December 13, 1985, available online at http://mn.findacase.com/research/wfrmDocViewer.aspx/xq/fac.19851213_0004.MN.htm/qx.

4 "Suspect in Bankers' Killing Found Dead on Texas Farm," *The New York Times*, October 3, 1983, p. A16.

5 "Man Convicted of Killing Two Bankers 17 Years Ago Confesses," *Brainerd Dispatch*, September 13, 2000, available online at http://brainerddispatch.com/stories/091300/new_0913000034.shtml.

6 Jeff Baenen, "Murders Blamed on Farm Crisis," *Associated Press*, April 28, 1986, available online at http://www.apnewsarchive.com/1986/Murders-Blamed-on-Farm-Crisis/id-8aaea00da020e55b476c8739bc745e85.

7 *Ibid.*

8 *When Father and Son Conspire*, p. 209.

A Mystery Resolved

1 Beth Hawkins, "Without a Trace," *Minnesota Monthly*, October 2009, available online at http://www.minnesotamonthly.com/media/Minnesota-Monthly/October-2009/Without-a-Trace/.

2 *Ibid.*

3 Dirk Johnson, "Kidnapping Sows Suspicion in Trusting Town," *The New York Times*, April 29, 1990, n.p.

4 Julie Nelson, "Conversation with Dan Rassier," Part Two, KARE11, October 6, 2010, available online at http://www.kare11.com/news/news_article.aspx?storyid=875817.

5 "11-Year-Old Minnesota Boy Snatched by Masked Gunman," Nancy Grace, CNN, February 28, 2011, transcript available at http://transcripts.cnn.com/TRANSCRIPTS/1102/28/ng.01.html.

6 Amy Forliti "Dan Rassier, Person of Interest in Jacob Wetterling Abduction, Says Cops Are Violating His Rights," *Huffington Post*, August 2, 2012, available online at http://www.huffingtonpost.com/2012/08/03/dan-rassier-jacob-wetterling-abduction_n_1736816.html.

7 "Minnesota man who confessed to killing Jacob Wetterling in 1989 sentenced to 20 years." Chicago Tribune. November 21, 2016, available online at www.chi-

cagotribune.com/news/nationworld/midwest/ct-jacob-wetterling-abduction-sentence-20161121-story.html

The Angry Heir

1. "Murder Suspect Talks to Police," *Cedar Rapids Gazette*, August 8, 1992. p. 15A.

2. Mark Neuzil, "Killings Put Spotlight on Lawyers' Ethics," Associated Press, September 11, 1992, available online at http://www.apnewsarchive.com/1992/Killings-Put-Spotlight-on-Lawyers-Ethics/id-0565e2fd0480dcdf29088dadcfb99295.

3. "Judge Sets Millionaire's Bail at $10 Million," Associated Press, September 1, 1992, available online at http://www.apnewsarchive.com/1992/Judge-Sets-Millionaire-s-Bail-at-$10-Million/id-56f38acb23b22f5c09e3b075a92b319e?SearchText=-judge%20sets%20millionaire%27s%20bail%20at%20%2410%20million;Display_.

4. "Grocery Heir Charged with Killing Wife and Boyfriend Commits Suicide," Associated Press, November 1, 1992, available online at http://www.apnewsarchive.com/1992/Grocery-Heir-Charged-With-Killing-Wife-and-Boyfriend-Commits-Suicide/id-0009bdf3629130c570711d053f0b3c3b?SearchText=grocery%20heir%20charged%20with%20killing%20wife;Display_.

5. "Official Mum on 'How' of Lund Suicide," *Cedar Rapids Gazette*, November 2, 1992. p. 3A.

6. Alex Ebert, "Killer Found Hanging in Stillwater Cell," *Star Tribune*, June 15, 2010, available online at http://www.startribune.com/local/east/96414594.html.

A Cold Case of Murder

1. Dee Depass, "Minneapolis Woman Missing After Trip to Mall of America," *Star Tribune*, January 1, 1996, available online at http://www.highbeam.com/doc/1G1-62901598.html.

2. Chris Ison and Paul McEnroe, "Police Doubt They'll Solve Dunlap's Slaying," *Star Tribune*, February 4, 1996, available online at http://www.highbeam.com/doc/1G1-62624383.html.

3. Chris Ison and Paul McEnroe, "Blood Evidence Scant in Search of Dunlap Home," *Star Tribune*, February 24, 1996, available online at http://www.highbeam.com/doc/1G1-62625361.html.

4. Margaret Zack, "Dunlap, Insurer Settle Lawsuit," *Star Tribune*, February 24, 1996, available online at http://www.highbeam.com/doc/1G1-62566927.html.

5. Caroline Lowe, "Cold Case: Anne Barber Dunlap," WCCO, February 2, 2006, available online at http://minnesota.cbslocal.com/2006/02/02/cold-case-anne-barber-dunlap/.

Amato, Joseph. *When Father and Son Conspire: A Minnesota Farm Murder.* Ames: Iowa State University Press, 1988.

Bessler, John D. *Legacy of Violence: Lynch Mobs and Executions in Minnesota.* Minneapolis: University of Minnesota Press, 2003.

Gorn, Elliott J. *Dillinger's Wild Ride: The Year That Made America's Public Enemy Number One.* New York: Oxford University Press, 2009.

Guinn, Jeff. *Go Down Together: The True, Untold Story of Bonnie and Clyde.* New York: Simon and Schuster, 2009.

Kimball, Joe. *Secrets of the Congdon Mansion: The Unofficial Guide to Glensheen and the Congdon Murders.* White Bear, MN: Jaykay Publishing, 2004.

Knopp, Larry, ed. *Queer Twin Cities.* Minneapolis: University of Minnesota Press, 2010.

Maccabee, Paul. *John Dillinger Slept Here: A Crooks' Tour of Crime and Corruption in St. Paul, 1920–1936.* St. Paul: Minnesota State Historical Society Press, 1995.

Mayo, Mike. *American Murder: Criminals, Crimes and the Media.* Canton, MI: Visible Ink Press, 2008.

Millett, Larry. *Murder Has a Public Face: Crime and Punishment in the Speed Graphic Era.* St. Paul: Borealis Books, 2008.

Millett, Larry. *Strange Days, Dangerous Nights: Photos from the Speed Graphics Era.* Minneapolis: University of Minnesota Press, 2010.

Norman, Michael. *The Nearly Departed.* St. Paul: Minnesota Historical Society, 2009.

Rubenstein, Bruce. *Greed, Rage, And Love Gone Wrong: Murder in Minnesota.* St. Paul: Minnesota Historical Society Press, 2004.

Siegel, Barry. *A Death in White Bear Lake.* New York: Ballantine Books, 1990.

Smith, Robert Barr. *The Last Hurrah of the James-Younger Gang.* Norman: University of Oklahoma Press, 2001.

Stiles, T.J. *Jesse James: Last Rebel of the Civil War.* New York, Vintage Books, 2002.

Swanson, William. *Dial M: The Murder of Carol Thompson.* St. Paul: Borealis Press, 2006.

Trenerry, Walter N. *Murder in Minnesota: A Collection of True Cases.* St. Paul: Minnesota Historical Society Press, 1985.

Woodbury, Marda Liggett. *Stopping the Presses: The Murder of Walter W. Liggett.* Minneapolis: University of Minnesota Press, 1998.

A

Ames, A.A. "Doc" 47

Anderson, Dick W.C. 104

Arbogast, Louis 29–30, 32

Arbogast, Louise 29, 31–32

Axilrod, Dr. A. Arnold 92

B

Bailey, John Harvey 48, 59, 65

Barker, Doc 65–66, 71

Barker, Fred 65–66, 69, 71

Barker, Ma 65

Barker-Karpis Gang 64–65

Bilansky, Ann 6–12, 168

Bilansky, Stanislaus 5–6, 9

Blixt, Claus 21, 23, 26

Blumenfeld, Isadora 81

Blythe, Rudy 142–144, 146–147

Bonnie and Clyde 56, 170

Bremer, Edward 64, 69

Brom, David 149

Bureau of Investigation 48–49, 58, 62–63, 67, 69–72, 75–79

C

Caldwell, Marjorie 128, 131–133

Caldwell, Roger 129, 134

Callahan, Kenneth 123, 125

Canfield, Ward 100

Cann, Kid 81, 83

Cascade Township 149

Castle Royal 45

Clark, Larry 119–120, 122

Clayton, Elias 38, 42, 45

Clifford, Nina 53, 55

Coe, Dr. John 94

Connery, Officer George 36

Crutcher, Oliver 87, 89–90

Cunanan, Andrew 165

D

Dakota Uprising 12

DeZeler, Arthur 91

DeZeler, Grace 91

Dillinger, John 48, 56, 67, 72–73, 76, 78

Duluth 33, 38–40, 43–45, 102, 124, 128, 130, 132–134, 136

Dunlap, Anne Barber 161, 164

Dunn, Frank 33–34, 36–37

E

Engeldinger, Andrew 167

F

Fossum, Officer Robert 100

Frechette, Evelyn, "Billie" 72, 74

Friedberg, Joe 156–157

G

Gillis, Lester 74

Ging, Catherine "Kitty" 3–4, 21–24, 26–28

Glensheen 128–130, 132, 134

Goff, Sydney 96

Grand Rapids 166

H

Hayward, Harry 21, 23–24, 26–28

Heinrich, Danny, 150, 152–153

Hogan, "Dapper" Dan 52

Hoover, J. Edgar 62, 65, 70–71, 75, 79

J

Jackson, Elmer 38, 42, 45

James-Younger Gang 13–15, 17

Jenkins, James 142–143, 145

Jurgens, Dennis Craig 112

Jurgens, Lois 112, 114, 116–118

K

Karpis, Alvin "Creepy" 64

Kelly, George "Machine Gun" 57–60

Kelly, Kevin E. 154, 156, 159

L

Larson, Don 123

Lee, Allan Lee 87–88

Liggett, Walter 81–84

Loring Park 126

Lund, Barbara 154–155

Lund, Russell, Jr. 154

M

Madelia 13, 19

Mastrian, Norman 104, 109–110

McCool, Frank 33–34

McGhie, Isaac 38, 42, 45

McQuillan, Alice 33, 36

Meints, John 28

Miller, Verne 57, 60, 62, 65

Minneapolis 15, 21–26, 34, 36, 43, 46–47, 58, 61, 65, 72, 74–75, 78, 81–83, 87, 89, 92–95, 98–99, 101–102, 104, 106, 109, 112, 117, 124, 126, 155–156, 161–162, 164–167

Minnetonka 154–156, 167

Moonen, Mary 92–96

Moussaoui, Zacarias 166

Murder, Inc. 80

N

Nelson, "Baby Face" 74–75

Newton, Donald 96–97

Northfield 13–15, 17–18, 20, 57, 61

O

O'Connor System 46–48, 52, 58, 72, 85

O'Connor, John 46, 72, 85

O'Kasick, Roger, James and Ronald, 99–102

Okabena 56

Olson, Governor Floyd 63, 82

Olson, Sara Jane 127

Orono 123, 156

P

Petters, Tom 167

Pietila, Velma 128–129

Piper, Virginia 123, 125–126

Purvis, Melvin 75, 80

R

Redenbaugh, Joseph 33, 35

Reed, Ronald 119–121

Roseville 55, 135, 137

Ruthton 142–143

S

Sackett, James T. 119

Sawyer, Harry "Dutch" 52

Sherwood, Jerry 116, 118

Shiue, Ming Sen 135, 140–141

Soliah, Kathleen 127

St. Joseph 150–151

St. Paul 5, 8, 10, 15, 20, 29–30, 32–34, 36–37, 43, 45–53, 55–59, 61, 63–67, 69, 71–73, 75–77, 79–80, 85, 87–88, 90, 96, 104, 108–109, 116, 119–121

Stauffer, Beth 135

Stauffer, Mary 135–138, 140–141

Stillwater State Prison 20, 26, 54, 97–98, 111, 126, 160

Sullivan, James 39

Symbionese Liberation Army 127

T

Thompson, Carol 104, 106–109, 111

Thompson, T. Eugene 104, 106, 109–110

Thulin, Toby 142, 145–146

Touhy, Roger "Terrible" 69

True, Della 85

Tusken, Irene 39, 41, 43, 45

V

Van Meter, Homer 72–74, 77

W

Wabasha Street Caves 45

Wagner, Abe 63, 80

Wayzata 167

Wetterling, Jacob 150, 153

Williams, William 40

Willmar 3–4, 57–62, 171

Michael Burgan

Michael Burgan is a freelance writer who specializes in books for children and young adults, both fiction and non-fiction. He also has written articles and blog posts for adult audiences that have appeared in newspapers, university publications, and on the Bloomberg website. A graduate of the University of Connecticut with a degree in history, Burgan is also a produced playwright and the editor of *The Biographer's Craft*, the newsletter for Biographers International Organization. He lives in Santa Fe, New Mexico.